Melissa

Eva Gibson

❋ SPRINGFLOWER BOOKS

BETHANY HOUSE PUBLISHERS
MINNEAPOLIS, MINNESOTA 55438
A Division of Bethany Fellowship, Inc.

Melissa
Eva Gibson

Library of Congress Catalog Card Number 82-71193

ISBN 0-87123-575-7

Published by Bethany House Publishers
A Division of Bethany Fellowship, Inc.
6820 Auto Club Road, Minneapolis, Minnesota 55438
Printed in the United States of America

For my daughters,
Beth,
Clytie
and
Leelee

A special thank you to my friend, Eileen Pollinger, for her critiquing and for the insights she shared when she learned to "wait."

The Author

EVA GIBSON is a homemaker with six children. She is active in a Baptist church in Sherwood, Oregon, where she teaches Sunday school and serves on the Mission Commission. She is a free-lance writer whose articles have been published in several youth periodicals. She has also written personal-experience articles for *Counselor, Power for Living* and other Sunday school papers.

Table of Contents

1. A Bucket of Sand 11
2. Star Flower 19
3. The Reaching Hand 26
4. A Warning 34
5. Creature of the Night 44
6. Found: One Guardian Angel 52
7. Scattered Thunder Showers 58
8. Melissa's Psalm 69
9. The Pink Dress 75
10. The Unexpected Happens 82
11. Broken Pink Dreams 91
12. The Fair 99
13. A Hidden Note, a Hidden Fear 108
14. A Guiding Star 113
15. Driftwood Beach 119
16. Hidden Treasure 128
17. Return of the Star 133

1 / A Bucket of Sand

It was the sound of screeching sand that wakened me—or almost. The dream kept pulling me back and I had to run. Salal bushes and tangled underbrush scratched my bare arms and legs. Sharp bare juniper branches came at me out of the darkness and tore at my flimsy nightgown.

I broke loose from the path fenced in with the bristly underbrush and ran down the endless sands of Driftwood Beach. I ran, trying to elude an unknown enemy.

The sand beneath my toes squeaked in agony, and I could hear my pursuer's loud breathing. Sea gulls, startled from their roosting places on nearby driftwood, flew crazily into the night, their shrill "meow" cries changing unexplainably into my own name. "Melissa! Melissa!" And it was Colleen's voice calling—calling. Just as icy fingers touched my back, I yelled and wakened.

I sat up. A breeze from the high open window touched my dampened nightgown and I shivered.

Memory flooded me. I wasn't on the beach. I was here in my sister's room and she was gone. Gone, without a word, without a trace. Her perfume bottles catching the glint of the street light from outside the window, her scattered clothing making dark, mysterious humps, were silent reminders.

And then I heard it—a light, scratching sound just outside the window. Like squeaking sand, I thought, and the dream terror was suddenly upon me. A crinkly feeling crawled over my scalp. I clutched my warm blanket for reassurance, and told myself it was only a part of the dream. But it wasn't. The squeaking noise continued and then—there was movement beneath the billowing curtain.

My heart pounded wildly as an object was slowly lowered into the room. "It can't be—" I whispered. I worked to gather courage. I pushed my blanket back with an unsteady hand and tiptoed over to the window.

Cautiously, I pushed the curtain aside and peered into the bright moonlight. I saw a boy walking away across the lawn. He turned, just once, and I knew I'd never seen him before. He had dark hair and a thick, square body. I caught a glimpse of beautiful teeth gleaming in a face that suddenly crinkled with humor.

The curtain dropped from my fingers. A car motor roared, a door slammed. I jerked the curtain aside again and leaned far out into the night—washed of all color beneath a moon-white sky. There was nothing. Only the thick bushes at the corner would have been able to see what kind of car left so suddenly after completing so strange an errand.

What was that errand anyway? I pulled the window shut and looked at the object at my feet. It was a bucket, the kind a child uses at the beach, and it was heavy, full of sand. I could feel its clinging roughness on my fingertips.

I carried it over to Colleen's lamp. In its warm homey glow, the bucket looked quite ordinary. Orange and green starfish chased each other around its dented sides and a thin yellow cord dangled from its handle. Its content was most definitely plain gray sand of the sandbox variety.

As I put it on Colleen's dressing table, I caught a glimpse of myself in the mirror; frightened, wide gray eyes were fringed with smoky dark lashes, tremulous lips were surrounded by whitened skin.

My hair—was brown. I gave a sigh of relief and visibly relaxed. For one wild moment I'd wondered. There had been such prickly feelings at the roots of it that I'd almost imagined it had turned white as Granddad once told me happened to his buddy after a night of terror in World War I. But the only white about me was my thin ruffled nightie that somehow made me look more like fourteen than almost seventeen.

My trembling fingers traced the edge of the bucket thoughtfully as Colleen's senior picture laughed at me reassuringly. "Dear Colleen," I thought aloud. "How beautiful you are—all laughter, and blue and gold. I know why everyone calls you Sunshine."

But the girl in the picture, dimpling with her own special free spirit, didn't answer. "Oh, Colleen," I whispered, "Where are you? Did you go because you wanted to go, or did someone make you go?" I searched her face for a clue but there was nothing. Nothing.

At last I turned out the light and crept into bed. Horrid thoughts came flying at me then like vultures eager for their prey. I could see Colleen being forced into a car by dirty hoodlums with shiny knives. I could see her raped and lying half-naked in a ditch.

"Oh, God!" I cried and I could hear the agony in my voice. Over and over again I said it until at last tears came. And then, just as darkness began to lighten into a new day, I fell asleep.

I sat at the breakfast table, looking out at the morning. Dew still shimmered on the lawn. The climbing white roses, flushed with a pinkish tint, spilled their blossoms on the ground, and glistened against their dark fir background. Indeed, the entire world seemed sparkling and alive.

Was it because of the fearful past night? Was it because of the sharp contrast of my nightmare to the bright morning that excited me? I didn't know. I looked up. The wide beams on the ceiling above seemed almost like protecting, shielding arms.

I felt a sudden rush of love for my home. It was an older home, the last one on a dead-end street. Its shingles were woodsy brown and a porch ran around three sides, two of which faced into tall firs, leafy maples and alders. That's why we named it Edgewood.

The house's interior fit our family. The big living room had windows that looked into the woods. So did the kitchen window over the sink, my own bedroom window, and the dining room one. Colleen's bedroom was at the front of the house next to the bathroom. Beyond that was the tiny bedroom that just fit my eight-year-old brother, Darryl.

Upstairs were two big rooms, one my parents used as a bedroom, the other we laughingly called, "Mom's mystery room," because everything ended up there in heaps and no one, not even Mother, knew for sure what was in there.

I heard the soft pad of Mother's felt slippers. She stopped at the table—a slight, attractive woman, with reddish brown hair framing her face in becoming little wisps. This morning there were dark smudges beneath her eyes and her face seemed pale.

She looked at me searchingly and I felt sure her eyes had closed but little that night. A sudden stab of love that was pure pain flooded me. Impulsively I stood up and put my arms around her. She held me so tightly I thought I could feel a faint vibration coursing through her. I knew it was from sadness.

As we drew apart, she touched my cheek. "I wonder if it was a good idea for you to sleep in Colleen's room last night," she said. The worry crinkle between her brows deepened. "Perhaps it made this situation too close and real for you."

I shook my head. "It was something I had to do, Mother."

She nodded. "I understand, Melissa. Did you get any rest at all?"

"Yes. After the nightmare."

"Colleen?"

"I could hear her voice calling me. I was running and running. Somebody was chasing me."

Mother went over to the refrigerator, her bright pink bathrobe bringing out the dawn tints in her hair. She took out a carton of eggs, the milk and margarine. "It was a hard night for me too," she confessed. "I kept listening for her footsteps. Once I heard a car door slam, and thought, 'She's home!' but it was nothing."

Excitement welled up inside me. "Did you see the car?" I asked.

"Yes. I got out of bed and went to the window. It was parked on the other side of the street. By the time I got there it was starting to leave."

"What did it look like?"

"Oh, it was sort of whitish-colored, an older car, I guess. Not too big."

"What kind?"

"Why, Melissa, I don't know. Anyway, what does it matter? Colleen didn't come home in it."

I turned away, my excitement dying. The bright sunshine pouring over the red-checkered tablecloth mocked me. My throat ached. I went over to the cupboard and began pulling down glasses. "Plates?" I asked.

"Yes. We're having scrambled eggs. You can help with the toast if you like."

Darryl came into the kitchen. "Has Colleen come home yet?" he asked.

"No," I told him. I handed him plates and forks. "Take these to the table. Then I can start the toast."

"But why hasn't Colleen come home?" he wanted to know, his blue eyes wide and filled with concern.

"Why don't you brush your hair?" I asked. "It's sticking straight up all over."

"Melissa," Mother gently reproved. She went over to Darryl and put her arms around his pajamed figure. For a moment his face burrowed into the depths of her fuzzy robe. "We don't know why Colleen hasn't come home, Son. But we do know that Jesus knows, and cares about her even more than we do. She's in good hands."

"But if she's in Jesus' hands, why are you both looking so awful?" he persisted.

My eyes met Mother's over Darryl's tousled hair. "I guess we forget it sometimes," she said slowly. "Especially at night when darkness comes."

In the thoughtful silence that followed, my eyes sought the plaque over the table. "In all thy ways acknowledge Him, and He shall direct thy paths." Would He direct Colleen's path? I didn't know. I only knew my own carefree path had suddenly become full of dark and frightening places I had never before dreamed existed.

Mother's voice broke into my troubled reverie. "Daddy called late last night. He'll be home from the sales conference this afternoon."

A quiet thankfulness overwhelmed me. I drew a deep breath. "Maybe he'll be able to figure out where Colleen went."

"Or at least know what to do next," Mother said. "I asked him if we should call the police. He thinks we should wait until he gets home."

"Why?" I demanded. "I'd think the sooner the better, if she's in real trouble."

"Daddy says that with so many kids running away they can't possibly do anything besides file a report."

I could understand that. I made a quick side trip down the freeway in my imagination: girls with their thumbs out, couples resting on backpacks, guys in shorts holding up cardboard placards.

Suddenly, the door opened and Dad was there. "You're early!" Mother cried, and I thought I heard tears in her voice.

Relief flooded me. "Dad!" He stood, his shoulders squared with concern. So reassuring he was, so calm; yet caring filled his dark blue eyes and spilled out with his words.

"We'll do everything we can to find her, everything. And we will. We will."

His strong arm was pulling Darryl close, his hand rested on my head. And then he had Mother in his arms, comforting and soothing her.

I grabbed Darryl's hand and dragged him into the living room.

"What'd you do that for?" he demanded.

"Mother needs him more right now than we do," I explained.

"But I'm hungry," he complained.

"Go pick some flowers for the breakfast table," I suggested abruptly.

I went into my room and tossed my blue robe on the bed. Jeans and my favorite knit top would do. As I pulled them on, I admired my room. I'd redecorated it last semester as part of the home-decorating course I'd taken. I wasn't tired of it, yet.

The thick, mossy green rugs on the hardwood floor, drapes and spread printed with green trees and a grouping of graceful deer made it look woodsy. My maple desk and bureau gleamed with fresh polish. I'd even painted the ceiling sky blue.

There was a lovely water-color Colleen had done for me when I'd redecorated. It was a deer standing in a little leafy glade, its nostrils about to quiver, its white tail a flag. It looked like it was ready to flee.

I smoothed the bumps out of the pillow and just fussed around for awhile. When I thought Mom and Dad had had enough time alone, I went back into the kitchen. Neither of them were there, but Darryl was. And he wasn't alone either! Not if you counted the flaming fireweed piled high on the table!

"Where did you get all that?" I gasped.

His hands were busy arranging and rearranging his giant contribution. "It's all over out in the cleared area in the woods. Do you think they'll be surprised?"

"Oh, they'll be surprised all right," I retorted. "You've got an awful lot here!"

"I know. But there's so much, I didn't know how to choose, so I just brought a bunch."

"I'll help." I went into the kitchen and found an old, lidless aluminum coffeepot Mother had saved for bouquets. She said it had an artistic looking spout.

I filled it with water and brought it to Darryl. Together we sorted out the prettiest and arranged them in it. Darryl picked out his favorite and stuck it at a rakish angle in the spout. It really looked quite good.

"But what shall we do with the rest?" Darryl wanted to know.

I scratched my head. "I know," I said. "We'll take them outside and pretend to have a great bonfire. After all, it's fireweed."

"Why do they call it that?"

"Daddy says it's because it looks like a flaming fire torch, and Mother says it's because after there's a fire in the forest, these are the first things to grow."

"Who's right?"

"I don't know. Maybe they both are."

When the fireweed had been carried away, we set the table. I think the flaming weed did make Mom and Dad feel better because over breakfast they talked about the woodland flowers they'd enjoyed as children. Dad said his favorites were the wild purple violets that grew beside the creek near his country home.

"But they're such shy things," I protested in surprise. "Not like you at all."

Dad grinned. "And why not?"

"Oh, I don't know," I mumbled, "you're so tall—so oh, I don't know, for sure—"

Dad leaned back, his dark brows furrowing over suddenly thoughtful eyes. "People aren't always what they seem on the outside, Little One—"

"Dandelions are my favorites!" Darryl exclaimed.

Everyone laughed. It was better than worrying over Colleen, I was sure.

After breakfast, Mother asked me to help her go through Colleen's room. "Daddy asked me to," she explained. "I hate to do it. It seems so prying somehow, especially since Colleen is nineteen." She sighed audibly. "But he thinks we might find a clue. I'll feel better with you there, not quite so much the snoopy, suspicious mother." I could understand how she felt.

It was hard to open the door and be reminded of my fears in the night. The room's gold and cream and powder blue were in direct contrast to a dark and fearful sand-filled beach. Pale yellow curtains swayed in a gentle breeze. A sea gull mobile flew noiselessly round and round. "Seven sea gulls flying," I murmured as I touched their gleaming golden wings.

"If one has a difficult job, the best thing to do is just dive in and do it," Mother said briskly.

Together we dove in and did. We rummaged through bureau drawers and closet shelves. I even searched the pockets of the garments hanging in the closet. There was nothing. Only a few wads of Kleenex, a comb, and a couple of dimes.

"I don't think she's taken any of her clothes," Mother said in a voice taut with concern.

"I know she kept a diary," I said, and instantly felt like a traitor. "Of course, she may have taken it with her."

Mother slid her hand under the pillow. Then she got down on her hands and knees and began pushing the shoes and stuff that had been jammed beneath the bed.

To this day I don't know why I did what I did then. I went over to the bed and slid my hand under the mattress. My fingers touched the thin pages of a notebook. There was no doubt in my mind that it was my sister's diary. Keeping one eye on Mother's back, I pulled it out and shoved it inside the front of my jeans. It felt cool and hard pressed against my stomach. I felt guilty.

"Nothing there but a mess," Mother said with disgust. She got up and brushed off her knees and hands. Then she did what I had done, only much more vigorously. Both ends and sides of the mattress were lifted and bounced back into place.

"Well, that's that." She smoothed the bed and then picked up the sand bucket I had left on the dressing table. "Darryl sure leaves things in the funniest places," she observed.

"I'll take it to the sandbox," I offered, anxious to get away with my stiff, unyielding waistline.

"Thanks," she murmured. "We're finished anyway."

If only we were, I thought as I went through the house and out the back door.

Darryl's sandbox was really an old boat filled with sand. It was in the far corner of the yard surrounded by rhododendrons, fuchsias and tall purple foxgloves. The only way to get there was by a little rock path edged with violets and ferns. Once there, I was enclosed in a world apart.

If Darryl or his friends weren't there, I'd sometimes come and just dream, or read, or think things through—sometimes with God, sometimes by myself. Today it would be Colleen and me.

I tossed the diary onto the boat seat and sat down. Absently I pushed my fingers into the sand in the bucket. I felt something hard and sharp.

"Melissa! Melissa!" Was there urgency in Mother's call? I shoved the bucket and diary as far under the prow as I could reach and ran back into the house.

2 / Star Flower

Mother put the phone down as I came through the door. "That was Mrs. Wilson," she explained. "She needs you to baby-sit right away. Her mother is in the hospital."

"But Mother," I wailed, "I don't want to baby-sit today!"

"Nonsense, Melissa. You need the money."

"Some things are more important than money! You've said that yourself!" I took a deep breath. "Besides, you've never baby-sat Tad and Judith! They are the most boring kids I know. And that house is always a mess!"

"Melissa!" Mother reproved.

I stared at her, feeling young and rebellious and ugly all at the same time. "You say I need the money?" I challenged.

"I guess I said the wrong thing." She put her hand on my shoulder. "What I wanted to say, Melissa, is that you need to get busy, to be distracted from the disappearance of your sister, to think of other things for awhile."

I thought I knew what she was trying to tell me, but I wouldn't admit it. Instead I said angrily, "If you say I have to, I will!" I shrugged her hand from my shoulder and bolted to my room.

Bitter emotions tugged at me. Poor Mother! Wasn't one daughter causing heartache enough? But, poor me, too—baby-sitting, when I could be finding clues in my sister's diary!

I tossed a book and piece of unfinished macrame into my brown carry-all. The phone rang. I darted into the living room, almost falling over my own feet in my eagerness to answer it. Maybe Mrs. Wilson didn't need me after all!

"Hello!" I could hear the joyful, hopeful notes in my voice.

"Hi." It was a deep voice, manly, romantic, yet young. "What do you think of it now?"

"Of what?"

"You know—the jewelry—don't act so dumb, Sunny Girl."

I felt a cold chill shudder through my spine. "I'm afraid you

19

must have the wrong number," I said icily. "My name isn't Sunny Girl, and I don't have any jewelry. Good-bye!"

I hung up the phone abruptly. Mother came in. "Who called?"

"Wrong number. I'll be ready in a minute."

I ran back into my room and grabbed my carry-all.

Just as I hit the porch the phone rang again. I ran back inside and seized the receiver.

"Listen, Colleen," It was that same deep voice. I stood tense and waiting. "If you think you can play tricks on me, you're in for a big surprise."

My heart leaped. Maybe this was a clue. "What sort of surprise?"

"It won't be a nice one, I guarantee that." The handsome voice became dark and menacing. "Either you play your part of the game or—you'll be in trouble—big trouble."

"I don't think I know what you're talking about." I heard my voice turn tight and wobbly. "Maybe you could explain a little."

"I don't need to explain. Either you get the stuff to that guy and get word to me or you'll be dead."

The receiver crashed ominously in my ear. "Tricks," "Big surprise," "Get word," "Dead," beat on my senses like a dull pounding headache. I didn't want to baby-sit! I wanted to stay right there and see if that phone would ring again!

Reluctantly, I went out to the car, my ears straining backward, listening. There was nothing.

We were both quiet on the short drive to the Wilson's. I don't know what Mother's thoughts were, but mine kept bobbing around the events of the last twenty-four hours, and kept me wondering, wondering, wondering.

As I got out of the car, I asked, "Does Colleen's voice sound like mine on the telephone?"

"Not to me," Mother replied. "But to someone who didn't know you both well, it might be confusing. Don't some of your school friends get you mixed up sometimes?"

"Yeah. And I remember how Grandma used to, too." I started up the littered walk. "You'll call right away if you hear anything, won't you, Mom?"

I smiled an I-forgive-you-Mom and I'm sorry-I-was-such-a-pill smile, and let myself in.

It wasn't that I disliked Mary Wilson and her little ones. She was a pretty girl who could slip into the latest style and go out with the crowd at a moment's notice. But at home she moved about in such an ineffectual fashion that she drove me crazy. She'd pick up a sweater from the floor and toss it on a chair, stash a dirty paper towel into a paper bag and shove it on top of the refrigerator.

I never quite knew where to start when I was there. The sink was always piled high with dirty dishes, the counters were hopelessly cluttered. Behind doors under the sink, onions and potatoes sprouted hopefully, waving their tendrils in the damp dark. Every drawer would be jammed full of safety pins, rubber bands, papers and a queer assortment of utensils. Smeared baby food made the chairs sticky, and neglected baby clothes emitted an unappealing odor.

It wasn't that she expected a lot from me. Sometimes I'd try to clean up a little, sometimes I didn't do anything. She never seemed to notice—just patted Judith and Tad's head and asked if they'd been good.

This morning her pretty, pale face was tight and I could tell she'd been crying. She moved about aimlessly, pulling a baby shoe out from beneath a pile of magazines on a chair, finding her own jacket on the back of the couch.

"If you could take them to the park for an hour I'd appreciate it," she said. "They haven't been out much lately."

She moved toward the kitchen. "I can't find Tad's other shoe."

"Don't worry," I volunteered. "I'll find it. You go on." I picked up Judith from her crib and pulled her wadded undershirt down.

"I'll find it," I reassured her. I took Judith into the bathroom and washed the smeared teething biscuit off her face. Tad followed, his funny long train bumping at each step.

"Well, kids, we're going to the park," I said, even though I really wanted to stay close by the phone in case Mother called. I scrubbed Tad's round white face too. "Let's go to the kitchen and fix your bottles and find your shoes and socks."

Tad grasped my leg in a rush of enthusiasm and I suddenly hugged him tight. *Poor little tyke,* I thought. Then aloud I said, "We'll be ready to leave in a little while."

It was almost three before we got to the park. But it was worth it. I fixed Tad up with sand shovels and trucks and deposited Judith on the blanket beside me.

The canopy of leaves overhead whispered softly together, blending with Tad's contented car noises. Judith cooed and gurgled and I lay back in the dreamy green-gold sunlight.

My eyes grew heavier and heavier and I must have slept a few moments because when I opened my eyes, another child was in the sandbox with Tad.

I found myself staring. She was a beautiful child with sun-kissed skin, and black hair, dressed in a tiny suit of washed-out blue. She was obviously older than Tad's twenty-one months, but scarcely bigger.

It was like watching a silent movie. Without saying a word they busied themselves in perfect harmony. They carefully brushed tiny sticks and debris from around the miniature marigolds that marched along the sandbox edge. She picked a dainty sprig from a bush and planted it in the sand. With Tad's help she carried a bucket of water from the fountain and watered it.

If she were mine, I'd call her Star Flower, I thought. It would just fit her.

Then as suddenly as she had appeared, she was running toward the street. I leaped to my feet and peered in both directions, but no one nearby seemed to belong with her. I took a few hesitant steps forward as she started across the street.

"Star Flower!" I called. Then I was running as a car came toward her. The horn honked crazily, but Star Flower did not even turn her head. The driver skidded to a stop inches from the little girl.

I rushed to her and gathered her into my arms. She lay quiet against my shoulder except for a tiny quivering that reminded me of autumn leaves, frightened and about to fall.

The driver's face was suddenly very close to my own. "You crazy kid!" he yelled, "You should have been watching her! I could have killed her!"

I looked at him speechlessly and nodded, then turned away. There was an angry squeal of tires, a curse and he was gone. But I had Star Flower and she was safe. I would just keep her until someone came for her.

I carried her back to our blanket and sat her down beside Judith. I tried to talk to her to tell her who I was and to find out who she was, but she was silent, her large, expressive eyes following my every move. After awhile she stopped trembling and picked up a marigold for Judith. It was wasted on her, though. She mashed it up and tried to put it in her mouth while Star Flower watched in amazement.

I was wondering what I would do if no one came for her, when a dark girl about my own age came running toward us. Her skin and hair were like Star Flower's, but there the resemblance ended. Star Flower was petite and elfin, this girl was plain with large features and broad square shoulders.

"Leila!" she cried, "I've been looking and looking!" She turned to me. "How long has she been here?"

"Quite awhile," I replied. "She ran off once and almost got run over by a car. I brought her back here."

The girl sank down on the grass beside me. "How can I ever thank you?" Words tumbled out. "I've been so worried. I left her alone in the backyard. There's a fence there and she's never gotten out before. I should never have left her but—"

She pushed her fingers nervously through her dark short hair. "Joe was home and he's been acting so strange lately. Somehow I thought if I could talk to him without Daddy and Linda there. Anyway I went upstairs and stayed way too long—" She shivered.

"Don't punish yourself," I said. Hesitantly, I reached out and touched her arm. "I've loved having her here."

"It isn't that. She might have been killed." She looked at me and I noticed her eyes. They were dark brown and shaped like big almonds. The tears that stuck in her long lashes made her face shine with a peculiar beauty.

And then she said the strangest thing. "Do you know what it's like to have a sister you love just disappear into thin air?"

I shut my eyes for a moment and let the hurt wash over me. "Yes, I know," I said. "Believe me, I know."

For a moment I almost wanted to confide in this stranger all the hurt and agony of Colleen's disappearance. But I didn't. In the earliest stages of making friends, a wrong word can send one or the other rushing timidly away.

I looked at the exquisite Star Flower instead. I must remember to call her Leila now. "How old is she?" I asked.

"Almost four."

"Four!" I exclaimed. "How come she doesn't talk?"

The girl moved uncomfortably. "I don't know. She just doesn't, that's all. But she's smart, I know she is."

I nodded. "I can see that. She's little for her age, isn't she?"

"She's like her mother, Linda." Her voice tightened. "I'm like my mom. Dad married before," she volunteered. "Joe and Leo and I are his kids. Leila is their kid."

I smiled. "I know who Leila is now, but what's *your* name? Mine's Melissa Lloyd." I gestured toward my small charges. "These are the Wilson kids, Tad and Judith."

"I'm Elaine Richards. We live on Avery Lane, about three blocks from here." She glanced at her wristwatch. "I'm going to have to run."

"Me too." I stood up and began gathering toys and baby belongings together. Elaine got up and began helping me.

"Elaine," I said, "I'm glad to meet you. Maybe we could see each other again?"

A sudden smile transformed Elaine's face. Something about her mouth tugged at some memory deep inside me. *Why, she's almost beautiful*, I thought. Those gorgeous white teeth! Why did I ever think her plain?

Elaine nodded. "What about tomorrow?" She gestured to the tree beside us. "Same spot? Same time?"

"I'd like that," I said. "If I have to baby-sit I'll bring the kids. Otherwise I'll come alone."

"I'll bring Leila too. Linda works."

"I'm glad. I love your little sister. She reminds me of a woodland elf or sprite or something."

"I know what you mean." She took Leila's hand. "Thanks for everything."

I picked up Judith and helped her wave her chubby hand. "Bye, bye," Tad chanted.

Elaine turned and waved, but Leila walked on ahead, her small shoulders squared beneath the faded blue denim, her little legs moving purposely forward. But at the street she hesitated, then turned toward us. She was looking at me!

I waved exuberantly and yelled, "Bye Leila! I'll be seeing you!"

A light, joyous smile flitted across her elflike face. She raised her hand hesitantly and then—she was waving wildly, in delighted childish abandon.

I thought of the picture she made as I walked home from the Wilson's in the late afternoon sunshine—a mite of a girl in a soft, washed-out blue outfit, dark wispy hair blowing in the breeze, tiny turned-up nose in the middle of a face made for a mother's kisses. Beside her was a square, solid girl who at first glance appeared plain, but who turned into a beauty when she smiled. Behind them was the emerald green grass and tall stately maples. I smiled. I hoped I'd see them both again.

As I turned in at our gate, the soft beating sound of an idling car attracted my attention. Something inside my head told me it had been there for some time although my conscious mind had rejected it. I turned. About a block away was a smudgy white car, smallish, half hidden beneath an overhanging willow. Two dark heads were silhouetted in the window watching me.

An eerie feeling settled in my stomach. Why was someone watching our house? Was I imagining it? I turned and started to walk towards the car. Instantly, it roared to life. I tried to read the license plate as it whirled quickly away, but failed.

I ran down the path and into the house. I didn't want to think of strange things I couldn't understand, of haunting dreams and queer sand buckets that dangled from windows, and cars that seemed to be watching me. And I wouldn't! I dashed into my room and shut the door.

3 / The Reaching Hand

At suppertime I acted like a Coke bottle that had been shaken and then its cap popped off. I talked and talked. That is, I talked about everything except the scary things I wanted to forget. I gabbed about Mrs. Wilson's mother's successful operation, Tad and Judith, my meeting with Elaine and Leila.

Poor Darryl kept opening his mouth to say something but I didn't give him a chance. I shot him threatening looks, and kept on talking.

Mother was interested in my description of the delightful Star Flower. "She's almost four and doesn't talk? That's unusual. I wonder if something's wrong."

"What could be wrong?" I demanded. "She's surely not re-tarded!"

"I wasn't thinking that, especially." She poked absently at her baked potato, her gray eyes thoughtful. "You say she ran out into the street and didn't even look at the car?"

I nodded. "I yelled at her, too, but of course I didn't use her right name."

"I wonder if she could have a hearing problem," Mother mused.

Darryl's head jerked up, his bright inquisitive eyes flashed. "A deaf-mute!" he exclaimed. "A real live deaf-mute!"

"Hush," Mother said. "I mean a hearing problem that hasn't been diagnosed yet."

"In this day and age?" Dad leaned back in his chair. "I'd think that would be highly improbable. Another generation back, maybe, or even in an under-privileged neighborhood, but not here."

"That's just where you're wrong," Mother retorted. "Kids on welfare get good medical care because it's free. It's the lower-middle-class working people who can't afford the high cost of doctor bills and have the undetected health problems."

26

"You mean you think Star Flower really might be deaf?" I asked.

"I don't know, Melissa. I'm just wondering and talking. I really don't know anything about it." She got up and went into the kitchen for the dessert. "I'd like to get acquainted with her mother, though. Maybe there's something I could do to help."

Dad winked at me. "Leave it to your mother to ferret out the details. It'll be good for her, though," he added in an undertone. I knew what he meant.

I changed the subject abruptly. "A car followed me home today. I think the driver stopped, and watched our house."

My parents exchanged a look over the frosty sherbet Mother carried to the table. "Our little girl is growing up, Mother," Dad said winking.

"What do you mean?" I demanded. "It wasn't an ordinary car on an ordinary errand. It made me feel weird!"

"Ten-to-one the riders were a couple of teen-age guys watching my lovely teen-age daughter," Dad chuckled. "You just put your pretty little nose in the air and pay them no attention."

"Melissa has a boyfriend, Melissa has a boyfriend!" Darryl chanted.

I felt my cheeks getting hot. I wadded my napkin into a ball and threw it at him. "Dad, make him shut up."

But Darryl was already leaving, with a hurried, "Excuse me."

I turned to Dad. "You didn't see the car, so you don't know. It felt ominous, it really did."

Dad got up from the table and came around to me. His big hand rested gently on my head. "You've been through a lot lately, Melissa. I can understand why it could make you feel that way. But don't dwell on it. Things have a funny way of getting out of shape when emotions get raw."

I didn't say anything, but I felt a strange clash of feelings inside. Part of me felt irritated that he understood so little, and part of me felt comforted because I knew he really cared and wanted to help, but didn't quite know how.

After the supper dishes were cleared, I went outside. Rays from the lowering sun slanted into the upper branches of the dogwood tree by the sandbox. I went down the little rock path, tall ferns brushing my jeans as I entered the haven of quiet I'd been yearning for all day. Now I would discover what object was hidden in the sand bucket, now I would search for clues in my sister's diary.

I looked around the little enclosure, and immediately was certain someone had been there since morning. The sand was scuffled up as rough as a wind-tossed sea. I bent down and peered beneath the boat prow. My strange bucket had disappeared, and Colleen's diary was half buried in the sand. I pulled it out and brushed it off, praying that no one had read it. Her own sister reading her private thoughts would be bad enough, but someone else, unknown to either of us, seemed somehow traitorous and unthinkable.

I laid the diary on the boat seat and turned my attention to finding the sand bucket. I looked over the edge of the boat, pushed low-hanging shrubs aside, even retraced my steps back along the path. There was nothing.

I went back to the boat and picked up Colleen's diary. For a moment I wavered. Perhaps I should just take it in, unread, and hide it in my room. *But suppose she needs help?* a voice inside me asked. *Suppose you can find out something that will in the end keep her from trouble?*

Slowly I sat down. It was a thin book, spiral bound and totally unpretentious. Something stuck inside the pages came loose and fell into the sand. I picked it up.

It was a snapshot of a boy beside a stone lion, his arm resting lightly on its mane. Chris! I leaned forward.

The beginning of a summer tan tinted his skin, contrasting with the soft-burnished lion. I could even discern those rakish hairs in his right eyebrow that curled backwards.

My heart did an odd clump. "Chris," I murmured, "Are you captive to Colleen's charm too?"

Dad's voice echoed in my mind. "Another scalp for her belt."

"No, Chris, not you," I whispered. "She couldn't lead you on and drop you, not you." Then since there was no one to hear except friendly ferns and trees, I whispered, "I don't care about all her other boyfriends, but she can't have you. You're too special."

I turned the picture over. "Chris," she had written in flowing beautiful handwriting, "my ideal of a Christian guy."

I didn't put the picture back inside the diary. Somehow it didn't seem to belong there. I shoved it deep into my jeans pocket instead. It seemed to fit there, perhaps because the thought of Chris was solid and secure. He was president of the youth group at church and I knew he walked with God.

Slowly, I opened Colleen's diary. The first page was a drawing, a fascinating potpourri of color. I stared at it for a long time. It was a sketch of two hands, one giving, another receiving a vast array of gleaming jewelry.

Somehow she had caught the reflection of light from brilliant emeralds and rubies that studded various necklaces, bracelets and earrings. A gold tiara glowed with the soft flush of rosy coral. An amethyst bracelet of delicate craftsmanship encircled the wrist of the receiver.

The star pin intrigued me the most. It was done in intricate silver filigree. The details were amazing. Little swirls and curls throughout somehow emphasized its beauty and unobtainability.

I turned the page. And then, while the early evening shadows crept around me, I read. I could hear the calls of children playing, dogs barking, the distant sounds of a car. I read on. The first star came out and winked at me before I closed the book. I sat still then, and let the magic hour of dusk close in around my numbed heart.

I should never have read her diary. But it was too late. It was mostly prayers to God, and I had intruded.

I could hear it clearly, the deep cry for help. "She's so near, Lord," I whispered, "And yet so far."

My fingers tightened on the rough spiral edge. All through its pages was the pain and anguish of a girl trying to live two lives, one for self, the other for Jesus. My heart quivered, as I imagined her smoking a cigarette and crying out for God to show her from His Word where it was wrong.

She'd written of boys, some of them I'd never heard her mention before. And the kind of guys she'd been running with—a choking fear grabbed my heartstrings. I'd read in the newspaper of terrible things happening to young girls. Could they have happened to Colleen?

I thought of the picture of the jewelry. Was this a clue? Could she have sunk so low as to steal? Was that what her last entry referred to? My heart skipped a beat. She'd been working in a jewelry store the past few months. I read her last entry again. She had written it to God.

"Lord, I won't be able to stand there and look at all the glittering stuff and realize what a fool I've been. Sometimes I think there's something wrong with me. Every time I do some crazy thing I want to run and run and run.

"A new start, a new life, a new anything, and yet it seems like You say, 'You're still you. You will always be you.' I can't stand it, this terrible restlessness that isn't even me—or is it me? Oh, God, forgive me. I cannot always take Your way."

I leaped to my feet. I knew I would never be able to share with anyone what I had read, and yet, I needed to talk to someone. But all my girlfriends were away on vacations. I thought of Elaine. If only I knew her better.

I shoved Colleen's diary under my shirt and headed around the house. As I turned the corner by the porch, I stopped short. I don't think that if I had seen a ghost, or even Colleen, I could have been more surprised.

"Chris," I blurted and slowly went to meet him. His smile was quick and searching but didn't quite hide the worry lines gathering around his eyes.

"Melissa," he said, "Pastor Logan just told me about your sister. I'm sorry. You must be worried sick."

A horrid ache crept into my throat. "She's been gone three days," I whispered. "We haven't heard anything yet."

Gently he took my arm. "I came to see if there was any way I could help. Where's a good place to talk?"

I gestured behind me. "Darryl's sandbox. It's an old boat with a seat. We can talk there."

As I led him to my special place, an unexpected joyful feeling began leaping and echoing around my aching insides. It made me feel guilty, somehow. And then, as we sat on the boat seat, the night put her gentle old-fashioned arms around us and drew us close together.

I spilled it all out. My fears that perhaps Colleen had stolen from her employer, that she'd gotten involved with some guy who may have taken advantage of her. Oh, there were so many things that could have happened to her.

I told him about the car that seemed to watch our house, the telephone calls and the strange sand bucket that appeared in the night. All except the diary. I didn't share that even though it lay unopened on my lap.

The sand bucket seemed to intrigue him. "You mean you brought it out here and it just disappeared?" he asked.

I nodded. "I could tell someone had been here, too. The sand was all roughed up."

Chris took out his flashlight and flashed over the mussed up sand. "Perhaps they buried it here."

"Why would they do that?" I asked "Wouldn't they have just taken it?"

"Maybe it was someone else." He dropped to his knees and began digging. I got down beside him and began helping. But it was no use. Our fingers soon scraped the boat bottom.

"If they buried it here, it's under the boat," Chris said.

I giggled suddenly. "Someone should take our picture. I bet we look pretty stupid digging like kids in the sand, in the dark."

Chris laughed, then suddenly became serious. "Melissa, I think we should talk to Colleen's boss. Maybe just sort of feel around, to find out if he's missing anything."

"I don't know," I said doubtfully.

"I'll go with you," he volunteered.

We stood up, brushing the sand off our knees. Suddenly I thought of the drawing in the diary. Shyly I opened it, and showed it to Chris.

"Since it was jewelry the voice on the phone spoke of, I've wondered if there was some connection between this picture and everything that's happened."

Chris studied the picture carefully. The gleam of the flashlight made it look even more beautiful. The greens, reds and purples glowed softly. The hands seemed ethereal, more graceful than ever.

"But it's not modern jewelry, Melissa." He pointed to the tiara as he spoke. "See, that's not something ladies wear now."

"I know. I just wondered." I reached for the book, but Chris appeared engrossed.

"She's quite an artist, isn't she?" he said. "The details are amazing."

"I know." I felt a stab of the old inadequacy jerk at my insides. "She can do almost anything she wants to." A touch of bitterness hardened my voice. "It's the *wanting* that causes problems. I have to go in now."

I grabbed the book and then remembered the picture in my pocket. A hot flush rose to my cheeks and I was glad for the covering darkness.

"Of course." He was instantly contrite. "Your parents will wonder if you've disappeared too. I'm sorry, Melissa. I shouldn't have kept you so long."

"It's all right," I said. "I'm not really the kind of person people worry over."

I could sense rather than see his troubled look and I hated myself for blurting out those revealing words. We silently walked toward the house. At the steps he grabbed my hand. "Melissa, if that man calls again, I want you to let me know right away. Promise?"

"Why?"

He hesitated. "I'd just feel better. There's something about this set-up that bothers me. I can't explain it exactly. Promise me, Melissa?"

A flash of happiness whisked through my being. Chris was worried about *me*! "I promise, Chris," I said. "But not if it's midnight!"

Chris wasn't satisfied. "Any time of the day or night," he insisted.

"All right," I nodded.

He still didn't let go of my hand. "Melissa, I wonder if it wouldn't be better if you told him that you aren't Colleen. That is—if he calls again—"

"But what if he knows something that will help us find her?" I protested.

"Maybe so. But I still don't think pretending to be somebody you're not is very good."

I could feel myself stiffen. "I'll think about it," I said awkwardly.

I risked a quick look at his face in the porch light. He was looking at me uncertainly, and yet, his eyes had a faraway look in them that was disturbing, as though he saw something far removed from us. I squirmed nervously, and I think he felt it.

"Melissa," he said, "last spring my mother was awfully sick. Do you remember?"

"Yes."

"Well, during that time I read a verse that grew to have special meaning for me. When Dad came in and told me she might not live, I ran to my room. My Bible was there on the bed, open. I started to read, 'Wait on the *Lord*; be of good courage, and He shall strengthen thine heart. Wait, I say, on the *Lord.*' "

I watched his face, so earnest and caring. "Melissa, it had to have been God speaking to me, that's all. I read it over and over, and the most wonderful peace came into my heart. In the days that followed when I'd start to get scared, God just kept whispering that verse into my mind. 'Wait, be of good courage. I will strengthen, wait, wait.' So I waited and He did give me courage and strength."

"But your mother lived, Chris. What if she had died?"

"The message still wouldn't have changed, would it?"

"No—I guess not."

"Will you read it tonight, Melissa? It's in Psalm 27."

I nodded thoughtfully. He let go of my hand then. "About tomorrow, shall we go to town and see Colleen's jeweler? I can pick you up."

"I might have to baby-sit," I said. "How about calling me around ten? I should know by then."

He gave a quick salute and turned to go. Halfway up the path, he turned and shouted. "Any time of the day or night! Remember!"

I smiled and waved. "I'll remember!"

And I knew I would, even more than he had meant. I'd remember, all right. The hand he'd held for such a brief time slid into my pocket and gently touched the edges of the picture tucked there.

But that wasn't all I remembered. Later, in the stillness of my room, I read the verse he'd wanted me to. When I turned off the light, it stayed with me, whispering into my mind its promises of strength.

I think it helped keep away those ugly thoughts that had pursued me the previous night, for almost at once I slept. Toward morning I awoke. I heard the faraway bark of a dog—weak, pathetic somehow.

Another dog, closer, began to howl dismally. I shivered and pulled the covers around my ears. Dark thoughts came darting at me then. "Colleen," I whispered, "Oh, Colleen."

And then the verse Chris had left me pushed into my thoughts. "Wait on the Lord. Be of good courage and He will strengthen thine heart. Wait on the Lord."

So I waited—and at last I fell asleep again.

4 / A Warning

Darryl sat on the edge of the bed, slamming his heels rhythmically against the mattress. The steady thump, thump, thump pounded into my unwilling subconscious. Reluctantly, I rolled over.

"Go away."

The thumping stopped, but he still sat there. And then, another sound worse than the bumping began; smack, lick, slurp. I raised my hips and bounced the bed in fine style, but the smacking continued.

"Why don't you get up?" he asked.

"Why don't you go away?"

"I don't want to. There's nobody here to play with. Want to play Cowboys and Indians?"

I gave a bored groan. Reluctantly I opened my eyes. There he sat, unperturbed, his big, blue eyes serene beneath a broad-brimmed cowboy hat, his tongue busy with a monstrous Sugar Daddy.

I made a grab for the candy but he eluded me without missing a lick. "Mother know you have that thing?" I demanded.

"Probably," he said airily. "It's been under my pillow for two days." He eyed me speculatively. "If you'll play Cowboys and Indians, I'll give you a lick."

"Ugh." I rolled over. He came closer, and I could smell his sugary caramel breath. "I'll tell you a secret if you'll play—really I will."

"Go away," I said.

It was no use. He began racing around and around the room shouting, "I'm a pirate! I'm a pirate!" He gave a couple of war whoops that sounded more like an Indian than a pirate, did a handstand and landed in a heap on my feet.

"Mother!"

That was all it took. My pirate in the cowboy hat took off

through the door like an exploding rocket.

I giggled, and pulled the blankets up under my chin, luxuriating in a day not yet begun. For a little bit I even let my thoughts roll into an impossible daydream.

Today Chris and I would solve the mystery of Colleen and that sand bucket. I would do something very clever, I wasn't sure what, and Chris would look at me the way he'd looked at whoever had taken his picture by the lion. Together we would bring Colleen home and somehow Chris would be immune to her lively charm because he would be noticing me in a new way.

I stopped myself abruptly. "You're being stupid and silly, Melissa," I said aloud. "You'll never find out what is happening if you spend your time indulging in foolish imaginings." Then I giggled because I sounded so school-teacherish and proper.

I pushed the covers aside and let my feet sink into the dark-green rug. Softly I padded over to the window and pulled the drapes aside.

The dawn sky was pale blue, with a shine like the chime of a bell, fresh, clear, full of hope and promise. Darryl was walking softly and cautiously over by the fence. I noticed he had discarded his cowboy hat for something that must have been a cardboard fabrication of a pirate's hat.

He even wore a patch over one eye. Not an ordinary black patch, either. It was round and golden, gleaming in the sun, and seemed to be suspended by a chain wrapped around his head.

He sensed my stare and looked up. I started to yell at him, but stopped as he put a finger to his lips in a hushing gesture. Even as I watched, he bent down with a furtive motion and disappeared behind the rhododendrons. *I'll bet his pockets are full of Oreos*, I thought.

I turned away and focused my attention on what I would wear when Chris and I went downtown. It mustn't be too fussy and yet not too casual either. It took a while, but at last I chose a soft blue T-shirt to go with my favorite jeans.

I examined my reflection in the mirror. Nothing spectacular, but I did look nice. The soft blue gave my gray eyes a hint of blue, and my skin looked fresher, more alive somehow.

"Well, young lady," I said to the girl in the glass. "You are *you*, and you'll always be you, so make the best of it." I turned away, ready and eager to face the challenge of a day marked with an unusually exciting, unknown X.

After breakfast, I volunteered to vacuum and dust the living room so I could be close by the telephone. I think Mother wondered what was up, but she didn't say anything, and I was glad. I've always hated explaining, especially to parents who seem unusually dense at times. At least mine seem to be.

What a day to be vacuuming! I opened the windows. Sunshine poured into the living room. Gold flickered on the soft green ceiling and book-lined walls. A breeze, fragrant with roses and fresh-cut grass, stirred the drapes and touched my cheeks with the promise of all outdoors.

The roar of the vacuum sounded oddly discordant and so did the telephone when it rang. Swiftly, I flipped the switch and dashed across the room.

"Hello!"

But the voice that answered wasn't Chris's. I recognized its ominous tones at once. "Colleen?" A nervous flutter ran up my backbone. I remembered Chris's advice.

"This isn't Colleen," I explained, consciously keeping my voice calm and efficient. "I'm her sister, Melissa. May I help you?"

"Look Colleen, do you take me for some kind of fool? I'd recognize your voice anywhere."

"But you're making a mistake," I insisted. "My sister truly isn't here and I don't know where she is." My voice faltered. I felt an awful impulse to cry. "I wish I did."

There was a pause. I could hear his rapid breathing. "You say you're Melissa?" he asked. "We'll see about that."

I wanted to say that he'd better not call again or I'd notify the authorities, but I didn't have a chance. He hung up as abruptly as before.

I sat down hard in the wicker chair and stared numbly at the bookshelves without really seeing them. My whole world seemed to be going round and round, and there was nothing I could do about it.

Except—*call Chris*, said a little voice inside me. I grabbed the phone and began dialing. He answered in a moment, quiet, encouraging, telling me he'd be right over.

Oddly relieved, I leaped to life. My dustcloth sailed over the piano and tables as though it had wings. Finished, I flipped the cord around the vacuum at the risk of Mother's displeasure at a job sloppily done, and stowed it in the closet. I even took a moment to look in the mirror and whisk a comb through my hair.

Then I raced to the kitchen where Mother was wiping the counter tops.

"Mother, may I go downtown with Chris?"

The cloth in Mother's hand came to an abrupt halt. She stared at me questioningly. "You mean our Chris—the one from church?"

"Yes," I said impatiently. "I just talked to him. He doesn't have to work today, and neither do I. May I, Mother?"

"Why, Melissa." A soft knowing smile touched her lips. "I think that would be nice, Dear."

"Thanks a lot, Mom." I dashed away, eager to avoid any more questions.

On the drive into town, Chris seemed preoccupied. I studied him out of the corner of my eye. Dark hair edged his good-looking profile. How I wished I could have flashed out some tantalizing remark that would make him notice me! But my thoughts wouldn't gel and my tongue felt thick, plastered to the roof of my mouth.

What do girls talk to guys about, I wondered. Oh, I'd read books that told how to get the guys started talking, but right now none of them seemed sensible. I almost felt like screaming in desperation, anything to break the silence, when Chris looked at me.

"A penny for your thoughts."

I flushed clear to the roots of my hair. "Not legal. You'd be overcharged for sure."

Chris laughed. "I like that." He looked at me obliquely. "You're different than lots of girls."

"I wish I weren't!"

"Well, I don't. I like people I can be silent with and not get up-tight. You're restful, Melissa. Restful and genuine—you really are."

I didn't know what to say to that, so I didn't say anything. But after my nerves calmed down, I was able to make small talk easily.

I showed him the parking lot Colleen always used, but we decided to park where it was free and walk. It was fun. The morning was warm, and the sidewalks full of scurrying people. I forgot the somberness of my errand and began to enjoy myself.

"I like to watch people," I said. "I always wonder what their lives are like and where they live. Things like that."

Chris caught my hand. "I'd rather watch cars—especially ones like 280-ZX's, Corvettes—"

"I like the store windows, too. I could just look and look and never buy a thing."

"Yeah," Chris agreed, "window-shopping is fun."

"And doesn't cost anything."

"That's the best part, especially if you don't have any money." He pulled on my hand. "Hey, wait up. We're there."

I stopped. My stomach dipped as I looked at the sparkling display of watches, rings and bracelets.

Oh, Lord, I whispered inside. *Don't let Colleen be a thief.*

Chris's hand tightened on mine. "Come on."

The atmosphere of the store was plush and glittering. I took a deep breath and looked around. I knew the plump balding man, with the turned-up mustache, behind the counter. Slowly I went up to him.

"Why, Melissa!" he cried. "Are you bringing good news about your sister?"

I shook my head, hunting for words to ask the right questions.

"Do you—I mean—you're not missing anything, are you, Mr. Reko?"

"Missing anything? I don't think so." Mr. Reko's elbows rested on the counter. His fingers began twirling the ends of his mustache. "You aren't worrying that your sister has—how do young people say it? Oh, well, you know—taken any jewels?"

I flushed. "Not exactly."

"I miss your sister. Why, the customers would come in just to look, and loiter—and then buy." Twisting his mustache, he continued. "Such a beautiful, beautiful smile. She could melt the stingiest heart. Such charm—"

"We still don't know where she is," I said. "We thought maybe she left something here that might give us a clue as to where she went."

Mr. Reko frowned. "I don't like to snoop."

"But if she's in trouble, we need to know," I insisted.

"I'll check her pigeonhole."

He was back in a moment. "There's only a letter ready for mailing, and it isn't addressed to you."

"To whom then?"

Mr. Reko carefully curled his mustache. "I'm sorry, young lady. I wouldn't divulge that without your sister's permission."

"Oh—thank you." I turned to go, but Chris grabbed the conversation. "You have a beautiful store here," he said. "Have you ever had problems with shoplifting or break-ins?"

Mr. Reko rubbed his fringe of hair. "No, never. People in this town are generally law-abiding."

Just then a customer came through the door. "Good-bye, Mr. Reko," Chris said.

"We'll let you know right away, if we hear from Colleen," I added.

"Wait! Don't hurry away!" Mr. Reko called. "I just remembered. There *is* a letter for you."

"For me?"

He handed it across the counter. It was a plain envelope addressed, "Colleen's sister."

"Where did it come from?" I asked.

Mr. Reko shrugged. "Someone shoved it under the door this morning. I have no idea who could have done it."

"Thanks again," I murmured. "Good-bye."

Outside on the sidewalk, Chris and I looked at each other. "Open it," he urged.

My fingers fumbled as I ripped it open. Large bold letters leaped at me. DON'T EVER COME HERE AGAIN! I stared at it, stunned. "What shall I do?"

"Let's go."

"But what can it mean, Chris?" My fingers fumbled with the foreboding note over and over.

Chris shook his head. "I have no idea, Melissa. We'll just have to think and pray and keep our eyes open, I guess."

It was different going back to the car. My thoughts darted and dipped and I didn't even notice the windows or the people.

On the drive home we talked about it. Chris thought I should take the note to my parents and tell them about the unnerving telephone calls. But I knew I couldn't do it.

"You just don't know my parents. They're worried sick about Colleen, and this would only make it worse."

"Maybe so. But if I were a parent, I'd want to know."

"But Dad thinks everything's the product of my overwrought mind." I protested. "He'd never take it seriously unless I had proof. *Real* proof, not just a crazy note."

Chris nodded thoughtfully. "Then I guess we'll have to get proof—you and me." His hand reached out and covered mine. "You don't really think I'd let you be in this alone, do you?"

I didn't answer. Something uncertain and frightening, yet somehow wonderful, was welling up inside me. Later, I would take it apart and examine it, but now . . . it was all too new.

"Chris, at least we know she didn't steal any of Reko's jewelry."

"True. Melissa, I don't want to frighten you, but I think that grayish-white Valiant, several cars back, is following us."

I started to turn but Chris stopped me. "Don't look, Melissa."

I stared at him. "But why?"

"I think it would be better if whoever—if it is someone following us—doesn't know we suspect them."

My nerves were going ragged at the ends again, sort of like a frayed thread end trying to slide through the eye of a needle. I licked my lips, then bit them till they tingled.

"Chris, how about going off a side road? Then I could look and see if they're still there."

We careened into a McDonald's parking lot. A cold chill shivered through me as a small, gray-white car with a dark-haired driver slowed, then moved forward into the traffic stream.

"We lost him," Chris said.

"I wish I'd gotten his license number."

"He probably wasn't following us, Melissa. Was it your dad who said you had an overwrought imagination? I wonder what he'd say about mine?"

I didn't think the overwrought imagination bit was very funny. "I have a hunch that car was the same one that was watching our house," I said.

Chris asked if he could look at the note. Carefully I smoothed the edges and gave it to him. He studied it, then handed it back. "Not much to go on, is there?"

I shook my head. "I wish I had that other letter—the one at Reko's. I'd give a lot to know who it's addressed to."

"Let's forget everything and have a hamburger."

I pressed my stomach. "Oh, I don't know," I said doubtfully.

"A Coke?"

"A Seven-Up." We grinned at each other and went inside. Chris ordered hamburgers and French fries along with chocolate milkshakes, and I was glad. It hadn't taken long to get my taste buds rolling.

We had a gala time over the pickles, relish and catsup, just getting to know each other better. I found that he liked working at the service station a lot, but that he had college plans for the fall. He asked me what my future plans were, and I had to be honest.

"I'm just drifting," I said. "Next year's my senior year, and I don't know what I want or what I'm best suited for."

He understood that. "It took me a while too," he explained. "All through grade school I wanted to be a pilot, but when I hit high school I found that most of my interests were in the forestry line. That's where I'm headed now."

I watched him casually stirring his milkshake with his straw, and felt a pang of envy. He knew where he was going.

On the way home, we talked about it some more. "You have to take into consideration lots of different things when you're choosing a career, Melissa. Things like, what you like doing best, what your talents are—counselors can help too."

"What about God?"

"He's the most important, of course. As you build a relationship with Christ, you begin to see things His way. Not all at once, but a little here, a little there. It makes life exciting."

He was silent for a moment. "Did you read that Psalm? the one on waiting?"

I nodded, feeling suddenly shy. "Last night," I murmured. "It kept whispering in my mind, 'Wait on the Lord. Wait—wait!"

Chris's dark eyes flashed sudden joy. A tiny dimple I'd never noticed before sprang out in his chin. "It stayed with me too," he said. "And it got me started on something really special."

"Like what?"

He rubbed his temple thoughtfully. "I got out our concordance and started looking up verses on waiting. And I didn't just read them, I studied them, thought about them.

"Melissa, I came to the conclusion people don't really understand what waiting on the Lord means!" He slapped his hand against the seat. "Personally, I hate to wait; it seems an aggravating waste of time—"

"Like at the dentist," I observed.

"But God tells us to do it. And God's no time-waster!"

Thoughts of the long night vigils over Colleen tumbled through my mind. "Well, I'm not sure," I said doubtfully.

A frown furrowed his forehead. "Why don't you do it, too?" he asked. "I mean, take all the 'wait' verses and really study them—"

"Maybe I will," I said hesitantly. "Maybe tonight."

I mulled those thoughts around in my mind as we got out of the car and walked to the house. I invited Chris in, but the moment I opened the door, I wished I hadn't. My parents were both there, not that it made any difference. It was the looks on their drawn faces that caused fear notes to creep into my voice.

"What happened?" I asked as we entered the living room.

My mother's hand fluttered to her throat. She gestured toward Colleen's bedroom.

I looked through the open door. Drawers were upturned on the floor, their contents strewn in disheveled abandon. The bedspread was jerked to one side, the picture on the wall twisted to a rakish angle. But it was the mirror that cried out to me and held me in awful fascination. I went in and looked at it closely.

A gaping fracture distorted its reflective smoothness. I stared at it, my face two half-moons awkwardly fitted together with a disfiguring scar. My fingers traced the ragged edges. I jerked them away, as tiny red bubbles appeared.

A golden glint on the powdery blue rug caught my eye. It was a golden sea gull broken from the mobile by the window. One wing had been chipped off. I picked it up and smoothed it gently before slipping it into my pocket.

Dad's arm slid around me. "I don't understand it," I whispered.

"Neither do we."

"Has anything been taken?"

"Nothing as far as your mother can determine."

"Jewelry?"

"All she had was costume stuff," Mother said. "I don't really know what she had."

"I'll look," I volunteered.

Carefully, I examined the wooden hand displaying her rings and bracelets. Everything seemed to be there—but I wasn't sure. I looked into her velvet-lined jewelry box. Briefly I touched the white envelope containing her favorite amethyst necklace. Its familiar lump was reassuring to my fingertips.

"Her turquoise necklace," I blurted. "It was one of her favorites. I don't see it—"

My parents exchanged a somber look. Something in it made me bristle. "You surely don't think Colleen came back and did this herself?" I demanded.

Mother sat down wearily on the bed. Dad put his arm around her. "Melissa, we don't know what to think."

The finality in his tone bruised me. I couldn't think clearly.

"Did Chris leave?"

Mother nodded. "He said he'd call."

I went to the window and looked at the house across the street. The flaming petunias by the front door looked inviting and peaceful.—yet was there pain and heartache behind the closed door—like there was behind ours?

I dropped the curtain, the peaceful beauty contrasting too sharply with the pain burning inside my heart. Vaguely, I wondered where God fit into this.

"I'm going out," I said.

"Where to?" Dad asked.

"I promised I'd meet Elaine in the park." I headed for the door.

"What about lunch?" Mother called.

"I ate with Chris!"

They let me go without anymore fuss, and I was glad. I would see Elaine. Maybe we could talk. Maybe, just maybe we'd figure out what this mystery was all about.

5 / Creature of the Night

I wandered distractedly among the big trees in the park. Children raced along the spongy paths shouting joyously. I stopped at the sandbox where Tad and Leila had made their little garden. All traces of it were gone. Miniature roads ran here and there as half a dozen children with scoops were busy making more.

There was no indentation or mark in the grass to show where I'd spread yesterday's blanket. For some reason it depressed me. Was that the way my life would be? Like a cloud that drifted by, leaving nothing, no mark or anything to show it had even been there?

I found a spot a short distance away and sat down, bracing my back against a tall fir. Its rough bark scratched my back, but I didn't care. I lifted my head and looked up, way up into its outstretched arms and let some of its tall majesty and peace press into me.

A bee circled, droning in the sunlight. I watched it crawl into the fingertips of the purple foxgloves. My thoughts followed it into the scented chamber. Its wings were quiet in the smooth, protected world of the bell-shaped flower.

A scene from my childhood danced into my thoughts. My fingers were encased in the smooth foxgloves, my waist encircled in fern fronds tucked inside my belt. A large maple leaf, with golden dandelions poked into it, decorated my head.

Standing tall on a mossy stump, I'd sung and gestured to my tree audience. When I'd finished they'd swayed in a passing breeze and I had been sure they had bowed in admiration. I'd clapped for them as hard as I could and the foxgloves had fallen around me like purple snow.

It seemed so faraway, almost like it had happened to another person. Just then the bee crawled out and made a beeline to wherever bees make beelines to. He couldn't stay forever in a pretty, protected cocoon and neither could I.

44

A fir cone bounced off my head and I jumped. A laugh as sparkling as spring water brought me to my feet. I looked into Elaine and Leila's dancing dark eyes.

"You snuck up on me," I said.

"I didn't think we could. But you were so deep in thought you never even twitched a lash." Elaine put a paper sack on the ground. "I've brought a snack for us."

I looked down at Leila, then dropped to my knees and held out my arms. She was in them faster than quicksilver, her soft hair touching my chin.

"I'm so glad you came," I said simply. "I've needed someone."

Elaine pulled a box of potato chips out of her bag. A Coke for each of us followed. The hamburger and fries in town suddenly seemed like hours ago.

We smiled at each other as we munched our chips. I realized then how much I'd been missing my girlfriends.

I watched as Leila tipped her Coke and sipped daintily. "You have a beautiful sister, Elaine."

"You do too, don't you?"

I stopped right in the middle of a munch. "How did you know?"

Elaine smiled. "I just knew. Something in your eyes, maybe."

I swallowed hard. "I do have a sister, Elaine." And before I even realized it, I was spilling it all out—the hurt, the nightmares, the fears. Elaine listened, her dark eyes filled with concern.

"The worst moment came when I went to Colleen's room and saw that horrible broken mirror. It seemed so crazy—so unreal. Then when I found my parents actually thought Colleen might have come home and done it herself—" My fingers folded and refolded the corner of the chip box. "It seemed like my whole world was crumbling—I don't understand it."

Elaine nodded. "It doesn't make a great deal of sense. Just the same, I expect it will come out right in the end."

"What do you mean?" I demanded.

"There's a sort of bond between sisters." Her eyes rested on Leila lovingly. "I think your sister will come back, if she can."

My thoughts hooked on that phrase. "The 'if she can' is what scares me. Suppose she can't?"

Leila slipped her arms around my waist and put her head in my lap. Gently I smoothed her hair.

"I talked to Mother about Leila," I said, suddenly anxious to forget Colleen and the storm of feeling raging inside me. "She wondered if she might not hear very well." I didn't say 'deaf.' I couldn't.

A frightened look leaped into Elaine's eyes. "Did she think we should have her tested?"

"It would be a good idea. That way if she needed help you could get it right away."

I didn't tell her how Mother had said the most important years for the development of speech were between the ages of two and five; that if speech wasn't developed by then, much valuable time was lost.

"Maybe I'll talk to Linda," Elaine said hesitantly.

"Or your dad."

Elaine shook her head. "Daddy has too many other things bothering him right now." She looked me square in the eye. "You aren't the only one having troubles at home."

"Oh, Elaine," I whispered, "I didn't know. If only I'd kept my mouth shut."

Elaine's touch was gentle on my shoulder. "I'm glad you did talk. It makes it easier for me to share." She suddenly covered her face with her hand. "It's Linda and Daddy. I've been waking up lately and hearing them argue and fight. And Joe—he's been acting so odd, going off without any explanation—"

She looked at me, her eyes pleading for understanding. "There isn't really much to say except I think something's going on that isn't good. I don't have much imagination, so I can't begin to figure out what, but it scares me."

I smoothed Leila's hair over and over. "I wish we could pray about it," I said suddenly.

"Pray?"

"It's too big for us, isn't it? Well, I have a feeling it isn't too big for God," I said, hoping she understood.

Elaine seemed unsure. "I've never prayed. I mean nothing besides, 'God is great, God is good, let us thank Him for our food,' at meals when I was real little."

"Would you mind if I did?" I asked.

"Oh, no. That would be fine." She quickly folded her hands in her lap and closed her eyes.

My heart leaped in sudden fear. As I closed my eyes, I felt a tightness come into my throat. I cleared it noisily. Would I lose Elaine's friendship by my stupid suggestion?

"Lord—" I said it hesitantly. "Lord—we, both of us, well—we don't know what to do. I'm worried sick about Colleen, and Elaine is worried about her mom and dad and Joe. Would you please do something in their lives? Keep them safe, please, especially Colleen. And help Leila, too. Help her to start talking soon. In Jesus name, Amen."

I looked up. Elaine's smile was the most beautiful thing. "Melissa," she whispered, "thank you. I don't understand it, but I think God heard you."

My spirit soared. "Oh, Elaine! He heard it! I know He did!"

It was time for Elaine to go. Reluctantly we gathered up our snack remains and made plans to meet again the next day. I patted my foxgloves good-bye and told Elaine how I once had been a lovely lady with purple gloves. We laughed together, Leila too, her lively face glowing.

On the way home I marveled at how our lives were beginning to intertwine. Would I be able to share with Elaine how to become a Christian? At the thought, a lump of fear settled in my stomach. Showing someone how they could become a child of God was something I'd never done before.

My thoughts dashed back to Colleen, then settled uncomfortably on the weather. It was getting hot, and my blouse was sticking to my shoulder blades. I squirmed and thought about swimming pools and leafy forest glades.

At suppertime I set the plates out on the picnic table beneath the hawthorn tree.

"I think it's going to storm," Dad said. He stood leaning against the tree, a tall glass of lemonade in his hand.

"No clouds, yet," I commented.

"Doesn't matter. I can feel electricity in the air." And he was off on a long story of how the cows on the ranch ran with their tails high in the air when they felt a storm brewing.

I twisted my shoulders restlessly. I think I felt what the cows did—a feeling of waiting mixed with an elated expectation that stirred the blood.

I started listening again when Dad began telling the story of his father being struck by lightning. "He was coming up from the barn with two buckets of milk full to the brim. All of a sudden lightning struck him, knocking him to his knees. We came running, but all Dad said was, 'Look, I never spilled a drop!' "

Mother put a platter of hot pork chops on the table. "I don't understand that. If he'd really been hit by lightning, he would have been killed, wouldn't he?"

"That's just what he said, Honey, and just the way we saw it."

Darryl dashed to the table. "What's for supper?" he demanded. "I'm hungry!"

Mother moaned, "It's too hot to eat"; then we all sat down.

Dad looked at me, his blue eyes gently probing. "Would you say grace tonight, Melissa?"

We bowed our heads and then, while the hawthorn bent its branches protectively over us, I prayed for God's blessing on the food and for His protection for Colleen. Then I added a prayer that was all my own.

"Lord, Elaine doesn't know you. Would you help me to show her what it means to be a Christian? Amen."

Mother lifted her head. "What is Elaine like, Dear?"

I helped myself to a pork chop. "Special—" Sudden confusion swept over me. "Something happened that made me think she wasn't a Christian."

"Happened?"

"Nothing awful, Mother." I felt my defense rising and hated myself for it. I didn't want the beauty of that prayer in the park spoiled by talk.

Unexpectedly, Darryl came to my rescue. His arm shot out for the salad and upset the milk pitcher. As milk cascaded over the table, Mother leaped to her feet with a shriek, her lap a milk-pond. In the confusion, my comment was forgotten. By the time Darryl had been scolded for reaching, the table had been mopped up, and Mother had changed, I was through eating.

It was a funny, lazy evening. Chris called and I told him about the mirror and what Mother and Dad thought about it. He didn't seem any more impressed with the idea that Colleen had come home when everyone was gone and done it herself, than I had.

The evening felt long and stuffy and I wondered if Dad was right in predicting a storm. As I lingered in front of my bookcase, my eye was caught by a thick, dark red concordance tucked between Bartlett's *Familiar Quotations* and *Unger's Bible Dictionary*.

Remembering my promise to Chris, I slid it out, blowing dust from its upper edge. I carried it into my room and put it on my nightstand. It looked awkward and ill-at-ease surrounded by Grace Livingston Hill, Mary Stewart and Emily Loring.

By the time I was ready for bed, the storm still hadn't struck, and neither had the desire to open the dull, heavy book. I lay beneath my sheet wearing only a thin gown. A faint breeze from my open window wafted in the sweetness from the honeysuckle that grew beneath it. I sniffed it appreciatively, wondering why the night always brought forth its smell.

I felt tired, my legs like dead weights. In spite of the heat, I fell asleep almost immediately.

Then I awoke to the slow rumblings of thunder and a wind lashing at the sheet. I opened my eyes. A flash of lightning illuminated my room. I saw the pictures, the drapes, almost as clearly as day.

I leaped out of bed and shoved my window shut. Another lightning flash, and I saw the brilliant purple-pink of the foxgloves and the last of the crimson rhododendrons tumbled on the ground.

I got back into bed and pulled the sheet up to my chin. Another flash came, then another. After each one, the picture of my room stayed photographed on my mind in the darkness.

A dislodged branch began scraping the window; back and forth, back and forth.

Reluctantly, I got out of bed again. I pushed open the window, grasped the branch firmly and started to shove it away. Furiously it resisted me. I shoved harder, and then—a flash of lightning—

I gasped and let the branch drop. I opened my mouth to scream, but no sound came.

My hands clutched the neck of my gown as darkness descended. Had I imagined a strange, winged-creature of the night? I strained to see through the blackness.

Another flash, and I saw it clearly—a tall figure with unfamiliar, blurred features, cloaked in an all-enveloping black hood.

A chill rose up my spine and into the nape of my neck. A funny metallic taste filled my mouth and I thought, *This is what fear tastes like.*

Then the 'winged-creature of the night' spoke my name, and I recognized his voice. Courage welled up inside me as I realized it was actually a person dressed in a hooded poncho with a nylon sock pulled over his head. I strained to see through the rapidly advancing curtain of rain.

"What do you mean by skulking around my house in the night?" I demanded.

"I wanted to talk to you," he said, a pleading tone in his voice.

"I know who you are. You're that telephone caller who won't give his name. You drive a dirty white car and—" Sudden realization shot through me. "You write threatening notes and leave them under doors!"

"I didn't come to talk about that," he replied. Another flash illuminated us. His hand shot out and grasped my wrist. "You've got to help me."

I twisted my wrist furiously. "You can let me go!"

"Not until you promise to help me!"

Between thunder rolls I heard his rapid breathing. My thoughts raced. Could this stranger of the night help me find Colleen? He seemed to know something I didn't.

Another lightning flash and I photographed his dark eyes and broad shoulders into my memory. I made a quick decision. "I'll help you—if I can."

His fingers didn't relax their grip. "Where's your sister?"

"I don't know," I said impatiently. "I told you that on the phone."

He was silent and the fingers that held my wrist seemed to relax slightly. Another flash of lightning and I saw his head bowed, his shoulders slumped over the window sill.

"Do you have them?"

I wanted to stamp my foot. "What is it you think I have?" I demanded. "How can I help you if I don't know what it is you're looking for?"

"My jewels!" he cried. "My brother brought them here!"

"Are you calling Colleen a thief? Why, if she wanted to take jewels she would have taken them from Reko himself! She worked in his store! It would have been easy!"

"They were delivered here! Your sister has taken them and disappeared—or else you're hiding them, covering for her!"

"I'm not!" I shouted, glad for the rain noisily drumming on the house. It wet my thin gown and I shivered uncontrollably.

"Then let me search your room!"

Quickly I stood to one side and pulled my tightly held wrist. In a moment he released me and vaulted through the open window. I grabbed my robe and pulled it on.

A warm, golden glow filled the room as I turned on the light. He stood there, water dripping off his poncho, little rivulets running down his nose. He looked so silly, almost embarrassed standing there, that I felt a giggle threatening to erupt. He twisted to face me, his scowling lips flattened by the nylon stocking. I instantly sobered and jerked out a bureau drawer, upturning it on the bed.

I grabbed another, but his hand was on my shoulder. "You don't have to," he said. "I know now that they aren't here. They must be with your sister, wherever she is."

I started to protest, then stopped. What good would it do?

His shoulders drooped again. "I'll just have to find Colleen." He whirled around and started for the window.

"Wait!" I cried.

He half turned, his hands resting on the window ledge. "Well?"

"If you find her, will you tell me?"

"Why should I?" He started to spring out the window and stopped abruptly. "If I find her before you do, I'll tell you, if—you promise to tell me if you find her first. Okay?"

"But how can I get in touch—" I cried. "I don't even know who you are!"

He hesitated and then—"just put something red in your window. I'll see—I'll know!"

And then he was gone, swallowed up by the rain and thunder, a strange, pathetic creature alone in the night.

I stood there a long time staring out at the storm. Before I went back to bed, I touched the carpet where he'd stood. The dampness assured me he had been real and not some figment of my imagination.

It was only after I was in bed that the immensity of my fright hit me. Chills raced through me, and I didn't know if they came from cold or fear. My teeth chattered. I turned my electric blanket on high and waited for warmth and oblivion to reach me. It was a long time before I fell asleep.

6 / Found: One Guardian Angel

I stood looking out the window, surveying the effects of the storm. The tall, stately delphiniums leaned precariously near the ground. The full-blown roses were scattered in brilliant heaps at the bushes' feet. The tender young fronds of the honeysuckle drooped, waving their damaged newness like a tortured flag left too long in the weather.

The tall firs tossed their fresh green maxis and flirted with the wind. I felt my old restlessness creep over me. I wanted to be up and away, to drift into the woods and leave for a time the closeness of my room and my fears of the night.

Well, why not? I let the drape drop and began tossing my clothes on the bed: blue jeans, vest, a long-sleeved plaid blouse.

Next, I carefully checked the location of Colleen's diary. It was there, securely tucked under my mattress. I checked pockets and pulled out the nicked sea gull, the ugly warning note, and Chris' picture. I left the note and sea gull with the diary, but I put Chris' picture inside my Bible. The two seemed to go together.

When I was dressed, I went into the kitchen. No one was up. I put raisins and an apple in one vest pocket, some bread and cheese in the other.

I left my note propped against the napkin holder on the table: "Going for a tramp in the woods. Don't worry. Breakfast's in my pockets." I added an X for a morning kiss and drew a saucy picture of a squirrel. Then I left, softly closing the door behind me.

The morning broke in windy glory around me. I started running toward the woods, the earth soft and yielding beneath my feet. I lifted my face to the sky and rejoiced in its blueness and the big lumpy clouds pushing up around the horizon.

The coolness of towering firs welcomed me. Immediately I was in a world apart—my world, for I felt at home with trees around me.

A startled squirrel jumped sideways and then began to chatter and spit in a flurry of indignation. His back was arched comically and his frustration popped out all over him, from his worried look to his stiff, fluffy tail. I laughed at him, but it only made him more fussed. I could hear his noisy chittering for a long time.

Soon, I was past the firs and into the leafy alders and wild hazelnuts. Then, quite suddenly, I was in an overgrown orchard. Untamed blackberry vines climbed the sagging apple trees. Darling little firs made their own miniature forest.

I smiled. Right there before me stood the most perfect Christmas tree I'd ever seen. Sweet peas gone wild crawled through its branches and dangled there like ornaments accentuating its evergreen beauty.

"Christmas in June," I whispered. For a moment, the exquisite reverence of that special day was upon me. A robin dipping low over my head reminded me of angel wings, a night filled with song, and shepherds bending low over a baby snuggled in a straw-filled bed. The message of "Emmanuel, God with us," touched my heart.

Quite naturally I knelt beside the little tree. "Lord," I prayed. "You're with me. I know it. And because you're with me, I can know that you're with Colleen. Take care of her, Lord. Keep her safe.

"And, Lord, forgive me for doubting you, for feeling you've somehow let our family down."

I stayed there a long time, and I knew God's presence was there. He was whispering love from every tree and flower.

After a while I started toward home a different way. As I slid down familiar banks, I remembered the spot from last spring. It had been a hillside of exquisite beauty then, with lamb's tongue flowers trembling on slim, fragile stems. Trilliums had lifted pure, waxy faces. It was not yet their time for the purplish flush and gradual sagging to the ground.

It was different now. I saw no sign of the gentle lamb's tongue, although a few faceless trilliums, sad and bedraggled wandered through the wild strawberry plants and ferns.

I was getting tired. I leaned on a mossy branch and closed my eyes. A jay called harshly. I opened my eyes, as a brilliant blue dragonfly hummed close to my nose. "The fairy's chariot," I murmured.

Another sound, a soft whining, invaded my thoughts. "Sounds like a dog's in trouble," I exclaimed. "Boy!" I called, "Here, boy!"

The whining came again. It was quite close. I stumbled

through the underbrush towards it, branches clawing at my clothes and hair.

A big rock rolled under my foot and I almost fell. I caught myself and stared. An old rock cistern with crumbled and moldering edges lay before me. At the bottom lay a white, furry creature. "Boy?" I called.

Its head came up and I could see it was a dog, probably a mongrel. It looked terrible, its coat rough and tangled, its brown eyes dull.

"Why, you poor thing," I whispered. "You can't get out and you're starving to death."

It whined, its eyes taking on a look of hope. I looked around. Then, with rocks rolling beneath my feet, I lowered myself down beside the dog. His tongue came out and licked my outstretched hand.

Quickly, I pulled out my bread and cheese. His mouth quivered in expectation. He ate eagerly, his thin body shaking.

Hunger pangs shot through me as I watched him. I got out my apple and started to munch it, all the time trying to figure out a way to get the dog out of the hole.

It didn't look too promising. The cistern sides were steep and although it wasn't too high, I knew I couldn't lift the dog out by myself. I would need a step ladder for sure. Even then I didn't think I could carry him up. He wasn't huge, but he looked solid and heavy in spite of his thinness.

Suddenly, I remembered Chris. Could he help? I bent low over the dog. "Boy," I said, "I'll have to get help. Do you understand?"

He whined deep in his throat and then looked at me with the most trusting look I'd ever seen. "I'll be back as soon as I can," I whispered.

It was hard to get a toehold on the mossy rocks, but I did it and lifted myself out of the cistern. I looked down again. He lay there, a mound of furry helplessness. Only the faint quiver of his eyes showed he was alive.

I hurried as fast as I could. Bits of moss and brush were sticking to my hair and shirt when I pushed open the door. Hurriedly I dialed Chris's number.

"What's up?" he asked.

"Chris!" I exclaimed, "It's a dog! It's stuck in the bottom of a cistern and I can't get him out! Could you help?"

"Be right there."

I grabbed up my comb and rushed outside on the porch to wait. As I combed the twigs and moss out of my hair, I thought about my dog. What would I do with him once I got him home? I remembered Dad and Mom's rule, NO DOGS! As far back as I could remember we had never owned one.

But this dog was weak and starving. Surely if I fed him up, and they could see how beautiful and protecting—that was it! I'd tell them about the horrid person who'd come bursting into my room last night. Then they would know for sure that God had sent the dog to be my protection.

I felt a surge of happiness. I remembered the Christmas tree in the woods and suddenly I knew what to name the dog,—Gabriel, for the angel who came to Mary with the wonderful news of her baby boy. And now Gabriel would be my protector, my guardian angel.

Quickly I made plans. Together we'd sneak the dog out and then I would sneak it home and put it in our basement. Once Gabriel was sleek and beautiful and clean, I'd show him to Mom and Dad. By then they would be glad to have him.

I'd hardly finished my hair when Chris arrived. We collected a gunny sack and some rope and headed for the cistern. On the way I poured out the dog's desperate plight.

"I don't think we could have managed a step ladder in all this underbrush," Chris noted. "But if you stay at the top of the cistern and lay on your stomach and pull, I can lift from the bottom; it might work."

I nodded. "We'll try."

So we did, and Gabriel was so good. He seemed to know we were there to help. He didn't struggle at all when Chris placed him in the gunny sack sling, and lifted him gently, slowly, murmuring encouraging words.

I lay on my stomach, rocks poking into my ribs. I reached out and took the corners of the sack into my hands, twisting them so they wouldn't slip. I could feel my face getting red as I pulled as hard as I could. Just about when I felt I must let go, Gabriel was on the edge and sliding on the rocks. I grabbed his rough matted coat and hung on. Chris was beside me in a moment, pulling us both back from the edge.

Gabriel made a whimpering sound. I pulled him onto my lap and was pleased to see him make a pathetic attempt to wag his tail.

"Poor thing," Chris said. "He's only half alive."

I felt a rush of compassion as I looked at my new dog. "He's mine now," I said jealously.

Chris smiled. "He's a little toughie," he said, stroking the rough white hair gently.

Impulsively, I hugged my dog closer. "He's my kind," I said.

"He's close to starvation though," Chris worried. "You should give him some warm milk—maybe mix in just a little dog food—"

I stood up.

"I'll carry him," Chris offered. He scooped the dog into his arms and we both set out briskly, silently intent on reaching home.

In spite of my insistence that the dog was mine, I felt confused. Perhaps he should really belong to Chris. After all, I'd never have been able to pull him out if he hadn't helped.

"*But you found him,*" a little voice whispered inside me. *But what will Mother say?* I stopped and looked closely at the dog snuggled in Chris's arms. His eyes were more entreating than ever.

At the basement door we paused. "He's really yours, Chris. I could never have gotten him out alone."

Chris looked at me searchingly, almost tenderly. "Then I'll give him to you," he said, his eyes smiling into mine. I felt a quiver of feeling rush through me that had nothing to do with a scruffy, half-starved dog.

I reached for Gabriel uncertainly. "I had best face the family alone with this surprise," I said.

Chris nodded. "I'll call." And he was gone. I watched him as he hurried toward his car.

Slowly, I pushed open the basement door. I caught my breath in a gasp of surprise, and just stood there, my arms overflowing with dog. Mother looked at me.

"It's a dog," I blurted.

Mother just nodded.

"It's sick—I found it in an old dugout cistern in the woods. You didn't expect me just to leave it, did you?"

"Melissa, you know our house rules. No dogs. And I especially dislike your obviously trying to sneak it into the house."

I stared down at the dirty, matted bundle in my arms and fought back tears. "But Mother, it's starving. I don't know how long it was trapped in that cistern without any food or water. Please, Mother."

"Sneaking is something neither your father nor I will tolerate. I insist you call the humane society immediately."

"But, Mother," I wailed. The dog whined pathetically and struggled. Impulsively I shoved it right into Mother's unwilling arms.

"Melissa, that dirty beast!" The dog looked up into Mother's eyes, its dark eyes pleading, its body trembling.

"Don't cry, Gabriel," I begged.

"What did you call it?"

"Gabriel. He's named for an angel."

"Melissa! That sounds irreverent!"

"Oh, no, Mother! It's because angels are protectors. You know, everyone has a guardian angel, and I thought maybe he could be mine. You always used to say I needed two. Only he'd be the one I could see."

Gabriel's tongue darted out and gently licked Mother's hand. "What are we standing here for? This poor thing is starving!" She was already starting up the the stairs. "I'll take him right into the kitchen and give him some warm milk. Melissa, you find a box and put in plenty of warm rags."

I stared at her retreating back, and smiled. How dear Mother was. Somehow I knew she'd come through. She always did! Mother never said anything again about the humane society. When Dad came home I even heard her say something about it being high time we had a dog in the family.

All that day I hovered over Gabriel. I fed him often and whispered love words to him. The only time I left him was when I made a fast trip to the park to explain to Elaine why I couldn't stay.

When I got back, Gabriel's ears twitched and he sat up eagerly. "Gabriel," I cried. I ran to him and hugged him close. That night I woke only once and that was to give Gabriel a saucer of milk.

The next morning, his eyes followed me as I dressed. I put both hands on his head.

"Gabriel," I whispered, "you're my friend now. You're even more than a friend. You'll have to take the place of a very dear sister." I stopped as tears burned my eyes.

"Gabriel, something strange has been going on around here. Maybe you can help." Sudden hope twisted inside me. "You can be more than my guardian angel. Maybe you can even help find Colleen!"

7 / Scattered Thunder Showers

At the end of the first week, Gabriel was a completely different dog. And I—I like to think that I was changing too. . . .

Soap, water and plenty of food had transformed Gabriel, but it was something else that was transforming me. It was the time I spent curled up on the bed with Dad's old concordance, my Bible and notebook, that was adding new dimensions to my life.

"There are a lot of times we're told to wait on the Lord, Gabriel," I mumbled. "And there are promises, too. Isaiah says that people who wait on God get to be like eagles, soaring in the air. . . ."

It was good to have a dog I could talk to. His tail would arch in a perpetual question mark, his eyes would follow me lovingly.

We went for long hikes together—just the two of us. We left the houses and streets, and rambled along lonely country roads where spirea bushes reared furry, fuzzy pink spikes of perfumed beauty into the air. Sometimes I found my eyes searching for sand buckets in unlikely places, but most of the time I just enjoyed the countryside.

Aerowood bushes were adorned in dainty white lace plumes now. In the hot days that followed, we saw them quickly change into soft golden-brown colors that sent a pang through my insides.

"Her hair is that color, Gabriel," I would explain. And Gabriel seemed to understand. His tail would droop and his nose snuggle into my hand in sympathy.

Somehow the great aching space left by Colleen didn't seem to be so raw and painful with Gabriel beside me. And there were Elaine and Chris. . . .

He came to see me almost every day. He was interested in Gabriel and still concerned at the odd circumstances of Colleen's disappearance.

He was horrified that I hadn't told my parents about my unusual nighttime visitor. But I couldn't. Something in me cringed from it. Would they think it some apparition that came because of my preoccupation with Colleen? I didn't want to find out.

We liked to go to the park when Chris was through working, and play tennis in the long summer evenings. It was lovely there; the trees made long shadows over the green, and bright red roses climbed the wires behind the court. After we were worn out, we tossed our rackets down, propped our backs against a tree, looked up at the sky and talked.

We always had so much to say to each other. I even felt comfortable discussing parts of my "waiting" studies with him.

"Pastor Logan showed me something special about waiting when Mom was sick," he volunteered.

I tilted my head. "What's that?"

"He said there are basically three ways in which we wait; looking forward expectantly, holding back expectantly, and being ready and available."

"Looking forward expectantly—I can see that. But the others—"

"Holding back expectantly is when we should hold back and let others take responsibility. And being ready and available means just that."

"I don't think I understand," I said doubtfully.

"We're usable when we're disciplined, when we let God's Word change us, make us beautiful—"

He shoved his fingertips through the racket strings. "When I'm reading about a Bible character, I even ask, 'How is this guy waiting?' Sometimes he fails miserably."

But the next evening Chris was different. He seemed preoccupied, his thoughts wandering. I tried to catch his attention several times but it was only with an effort he even seemed to notice me. At last I gave up and just watched the last wisps of sunlight play around the trees. Gabriel whined softly and I patted him lovingly.

"Melissa."

"Yes?"

"I went to Reko's store today."

My fingers clutched Gabriel's hair involuntarily. He yelped. "Gabriel, I'm sorry." I smoothed his head gently. "Well?"

"Something kind of peculiar— His store was broken into the same night you had your visitor."

"Oh, no!"

"Nothing was taken, Melissa," Chris reassured me. "Just the

lock broken and some of his displays messed up."

"Chris, I don't understand. Do you suppose my visitor left here and went directly there?"

"It looks that way."

"You didn't tell him—"

"Of course not. That's your business. It just looks peculiar."

I nodded. My thoughts began to whirl in the old way, before I'd had Gabriel to think about.

"That letter," I explained, "The one in her pigeonhole. Was it taken?"

"Yes. That's why I went back to the store. Something about that letter seemed important. I don't know why."

"Did Reko tell you whose name was on it this time?"

"After a fashion. He said it was addressed to a 'Rocky' and then a first name for the last name, whatever that means. He couldn't remember it."

"Wow. That's not much to go on, is it?"

Chris shook his head. "Did she mention any 'Rocky' in her diary?"

I felt my face grow hot. "I'll have to look," I said awkwardly. Somehow I dreaded it. I flopped on my stomach and began pulling at the tree trunk's loosened bark.

"Chris," I faltered, "I hate looking into her diary. It makes me feel awful."

His hand was suddenly on my shoulder. "I can understand, Melissa. But it's almost all we have to go on."

"I know. I keep telling myself that some good has to come out of it."

A thistledown blew close to my nose. I reached out and touched it. It clung like I had jellied fingertips. "Look," I said. "This means good days are just around the corner."

"Where'd you get that idea?" Chris asked, touching its clinging softness.

I shrugged. "I think Colleen and I invented it. I don't exactly remember." I leaped to my feet, my face to the sky. "Look! Millions of them!"

Chris was beside me, leaping into the air. He held his hand toward me. Little whispering fluffs tickled my nose. I laughed and went running after more. We both did. Our laughter and leaps must have made us look funny to passersby but I didn't care and neither did Chris. Somehow, it put us in fine spirits and we laughed all the way home.

I sobered up in a hurry when I got into the house, though. Darryl was lying on the couch, a thin blue blanket pulled up under his chin.

"What's the matter?" I asked. "Are you sick?"

He opened eyes that were heavy and dull. His cheeks were red and there was a white circle around his mouth. I put my hand on his forehead. It was burning.

"I'm thirsty," he complained.

I hurried into the kitchen. Mom was there, pouring a can of orange juice into a pitcher. There were little worry wrinkles around her mouth.

"What's wrong with Darryl?"

"A 102-degree temperature. He said he felt tired, and the next thing I knew he was asleep on the couch. When I went over to him, he was burning up."

The ice clinked. "I hate to have kids run temperatures in the summer," she complained. "They always get so hot and uncomfortable."

"Anything I can do?" I asked.

"Just be available," she said. "Maybe if he gets restless, you can read to him."

I went back to Darryl. "Mom's fixing you orange juice."

He looked at me with those heavy eyes. "Could you read to me, Melissa?"

"Like what?"

His dull eyes sparkled with sudden interest. "Something piratey or maybe mysterious." He shut his eyes again. "You pick."

I went over to the bookcase and let my eyes run over the titles; *Black Beauty*, no; *Heidi Grows Up*, too old; *A Fish Out of Water*, too young.

"Read me the one about the kids that get lost under the ground."

I scanned the titles. "You mean, *Magic in the Park*?"

He nodded and shut his eyes. Slowly I turned the pages, my voice droning in the hot summer evening. For awhile, I too was lost in the strange adventures beneath the earth. When I noticed Darryl was asleep, I shut my voice off, and went on reading to myself.

Mom came in, dressed in a light yellow duster. She touched his cheek and smiled gently at me. "His fever broke. I think I'll leave him here, though. It's cooler."

I smiled, memories of my own childhood crowding my mind. There was, I remembered, something very special about sleeping on the couch when I was sick.

I looked at Mother then, really looked. In the lamp light with that thin yellow thing on, she looked somehow young and vulnerable. Tired too. I could see dark shadows under her eyes. And how long had her hair been showing sprinkles of gray?

Mother looked up suddenly. "Why are you staring at me like that, Melissa?"

"Your hair," I blurted, "it's getting gray."

Her hand flew to her hair. "It is, isn't it," she said ruefully. "I've been noticing it, too."

"But its beautiful, Mother. It looks frosted—"

"The frost is on the pumpkin," she droned. She reached out and rubbed the back of my neck. "Don't look so sad, Honey. It's bound to happen—"

"You'd better get some rest," I said.

"I'm going to bed now. I'll keep the doors open so I can hear him if he gets worse."

I stood up, then bent to touch Darryl's cheek. It was damp and cool. "I'll keep mine open too," I said. "Good night, Mother."

She smiled. "Good night, Dear."

I felt a warm, secure feeling slip over me as I slid beneath my sheet. "Thank you, Lord," I whispered. "Thank you for home and parents that love me." Sudden emotion choked me up. "Lord," I pleaded, "take care of Colleen wherever she is tonight—and Darryl too."

My thoughts drifted back to Chris's mention of Reko's break-in. I knew I should be looking for "Rocky" in Colleen's diary, but I couldn't. I told the Lord all about it, and my feet touched the warm body of my dog. I think my last conscious thoughts were thank-you's to Him for my special guardian angel.

I woke with the unreal feeling I'd heard an unusual noise, but the house was silent. Only the pounding of my heart disturbed me. Then I heard it again, a soft stumbling noise in the living room. Instantly, I remembered my uninvited night visitor.

I sat up in bed and groped for Gabriel. He wasn't there. Swiftly, I turned on my light. The room was empty.

I couldn't put it together. Gabriel gone without a sound, a strange noise in the living room. Darryl! I flashed to my feet. We almost collided, my little brother, Gabriel and I.

"Darryl," I whispered, "what are you doing wandering around in the dark?"

His eyes were like an owl's, blinking in amazement. "It's Colleen," he said, pointing to the telephone. "Hurry!"

I grabbed it. "Colleen!" There was only a horrid crackling sound. "Colleen! Colleen!" There was no answer.

"There's no one there!" I cried. "Oh, Darryl, are you sure?"

"Of course, I'm sure," he said. "She asked for you."

"What did she say?"

"She said, 'Darryl, this is Colleen. Can you get Melissa? I have to talk to her. There's thunder and lightning and I'm all alone and scared.' "

I stared at him. "But—" And then I noticed his cheeks. They were brilliant red and his eyes were fever dull.

Mother came in, and put her arms around Darryl. "Honey, are you all right? You look awful."

Darryl put his head on her shoulder and burst into tears. "She said she was Colleen. I know she said she was Colleen."

Mother's anxious eyes questioned me. "The telephone," I explained. "He must have gotten up to answer the phone. But when I got there, there was no one there."

"But it was Colleen. I know it was Colleen," Darryl sobbed.

"Shh—" Mother soothed. "Melissa, he's burning up again. Get me some aspirin and water."

I stumbled into the kitchen, my knees feeling weak. Had it been Colleen? If it was, would she call again?

Mother had Darryl in the bathroom when I got back. "I'm giving him a lukewarm bath," she called. "It's great for bringing down a fever."

I brought the aspirin to her and went back to the living room. I sat down in the round basket chair by the telephone and willed it to ring. But it was quiet, maddeningly quiet.

I turned quickly, as I heard footsteps approach. But it was only Dad.

"What's up?" he asked, his eyes taking in my anxious frown, my troubled look.

Briefly I explained about Darryl—the telephone call. "Dad, do you think it possibly could have been Colleen? And if it was, isn't there some way we could find out?"

Dad leaned back in the chair and shut his eyes; hopelessness crept across his face. "It's not that simple, Melissa," he said patiently. "Can't you see—"

Tears pushed down at my eyes. Hurt made my voice go unexpectedly hard. "No, I can't," I said thickly. "And sometimes I think you don't really care, either."

"Just a minute, Melissa—"

I rushed on heedlessly. "If you really cared, you'd do something. You wouldn't be just doing nothing—always just doing nothing!" I stopped.

Dad started to rise from his chair, then sat down abruptly. "Go on," he said heavily.

But I didn't. Guilt over my outburst began to grow inside me. The house brooded with us in silence, the only sound was the splashing of water. Twenty minutes later Mother and Darryl emerged from the bathroom. Darryl looked better. The feverish flush had disappeared from his cheeks and his eyes didn't have that awful, heavy look. After Mother had settled Darryl onto the couch, she came back to where Dad and I were sitting.

"Now, suppose you tell me what this is all about."

I shook my head. "I don't know much. I heard this noise and came out. Darryl was coming toward my room with Gabriel beside him. He said Colleen was on the phone. When I picked it up there was no one there. Just an awful crackling noise. Oh, Mother, do you think it was Colleen?"

I saw her glance at Dad; I felt rather than saw him shake his head. "I don't think so, Melissa. Kids get delirious with fever sometimes. Why, I remember when Colleen was just a little thing and was sick. She wouldn't even come out of her room to go to the bathroom because she thought there were monkeys hanging on the sides of the door."

"I know I didn't hear it ring. But something woke me—"

"It might have been a nightmare—or a dream."

We went back to bed. But not to sleep; at least I didn't. Even Gabriel seemed restless. He wouldn't stay on my bed. He laid in the open doorway, his nose pointed into the hallway, his ears cocked as though listening—for the ring of a telephone? Or—was he waiting for me to get up and make things right with Dad?

But I couldn't do that! What had Chris said, something about waiting, by holding back expectantly?

I turned onto my back. Was that the sort of waiting I was supposed to be doing right now? Letting Dad take responsibility for decisions concerning Colleen? "But he should be doing something," I whispered through my teeth.

I twisted onto my side. I remembered Rebekah of the Bible. She was looking forward expectantly to Jacob receiving the blessing and yet—yet—' She didn't hold back expectantly when the time came. She seized the situation with her own hands, barged ahead and failed.

Visions of Dad sitting in the chair, leaning back, weariness etched on his face made me sit up. I jerked on my robe.

Gabriel greeted me with a wet kiss and I touched his head for reassurance. "I know, Gabriel," I whispered, "I know."

Softly I went out. At the top of the stairs I groped toward my parents' room.

I knew at once they were awake. "Dad," I whispered, "It's me."

"Right here, Hon."

I stepped inside and reached for his big warm hand, and knelt beside him. "Dad, I shouldn't have said what I did. I'm sorry."

His hand squeezed mine tighter. "Want to talk about it?"

"No—It's just that—that—" I could feel treacherous tears lurking close. I swallowed hard.

"There's something I need to tell you, Little One. I've filed a missing-persons report with the police."

"But why—"

"They felt that the possibility of her having left on her own was very likely. But, if something awful did occur—like an accident or—" He stopped abruptly. "Go back to bed now, sweetheart. Things should look better in the morning."

I went back to my room. I didn't sleep, though, until the first rays of dawn crept into my room.

It was late when I woke up. Quickly the events of the night popped into my mind. I pulled on my robe and went into the living room. Darryl was awake, looking out the window, a worried frown on his face.

"Well?" I said, plopping down on his blanket.

"Mother says I had a nightmare," he said. His brooding eyes stared into mine. "She says a fever makes you think funny things."

"So Colleen wasn't really on the phone after all?"

"I didn't say that. That's just what Mother thinks."

"And what do you think?"

"I *talked* to Colleen," he persisted. "It must have been the lightning that cut off the connection."

"But there wasn't any lightning, Darryl."

"Not here, but there was there."

"And that's all she said? Just get me to the phone because she was scared of the thunder and lightning?"

"Yeah. I went to get you."

I squeezed his hand impulsively. "You did all right, Darryl."

"Melissa, could you ask Mother if I can watch TV?"

"Sure, but she won't care. That's one neat thing about being sick. Mom always lets us watch TV." I flipped on the dial and went into the kitchen.

Dad, Mom and I were eating our scrambled eggs when Darryl rushed in, his eyes big with excitement. "He says there were scattered thunderstorms up and down the coast last night. He did! He really did!"

I jumped up, my fork and knife clattering to the floor. "Who?" I cried.

"The weatherman!" Darryl exclaimed. "I know it wasn't a dream! I knew it!"

"Well," Dad said slowly. "It's not much. But at least it's something."

"But how—"

"I'll call the weather bureau and find out what towns on the coast had thunder showers. Maybe something will turn up, after all."

"If we could trace the call—if it *was* a call," Mother said doubtfully.

Dad shook his head. "It's not that easy. Anyway, let's eat; then we'll plan our strategy."

After breakfast we knelt on the living room floor, a large Oregon map spread before us. Dad made dark circles up and down the coast, then here and there in the Cascade Range. It was looking more hopeless all the time. To my overwrought imagination the black circles were swarms of black vultures swooping low, eager to devour. I turned away.

"Where do we start?" Mother asked wearily.

"That's not the half of it," Dad said. "There seems to have been a lot of thunder activity throughout the Northwest. At least that's what the weather bureau said."

I felt suddenly dull. The hope that had so eagerly sprouted was crumbling away.

"Mother, may I go swimming with Elaine? I promised—"

Mother looked at her watch. "All right, Honey. Wait! I almost forgot. I told Mrs. Wilson you'd baby-sit this afternoon."

"Mother!" I wailed.

Her look was gentle, half-sympathetic, yet firm. "Run along now. Just be back at one."

I felt like sticking my tongue out at her, but I didn't. *What is there about being treated like a child that makes a person act like one?* I wondered, as I ran into my room to collect my swimsuit, towel and suntan lotion.

At the pool, warm wind pushed through my hair and swept over my arms and legs. "At least there aren't any hints of thunder showers here," I said, and went on to explain to Elaine about the night's strange happening.

"I think it was just a coincidence," Elaine said. "I remember once when I was sick and thought a mouse had climbed into my drawer and died. Mother had to open it up and prove to me there was no mouse there before I would believe her."

I felt flattened. The silly little clues I'd discovered so far weren't really clues at all. The telephone call wasn't anything but a sick child's delusion.

I raced over to the diving board and dived deep, deep into the blue water. When I surfaced I turned onto my back and floated. The water made little ripples over my bright red suit and tanned legs.

"Come on in!" I yelled at Elaine.

But she only smiled and shook her head. "I can't swim!"

I turned onto my stomach and swam to her. "I'll teach you," I offered, and together amidst the noisy shouts of children and our own wild splashing, Elaine finally managed to stay afloat.

It was after one when I got home. "Hurry!" Mother called.

I raced to my room, threw my suit and towel in a heap on the floor and hurried into my clothes.

Mother was rattled as she always is when one of us is late. "I told her you'd be there on time," she kept saying over and over.

"I'm sorry, Mother. I was teaching Elaine how to swim, and I just lost track of the time."

But it didn't do any good. Mother kept on fussing and talking, and fussing and talking, until I was finally out of the house and on my way.

The little frame house was sweltering. Judith was teething, her palid face plastered with gummy teething biscuits.

Mrs. Wilson loitered in the living room. "I won't be long," she said. "But I need nylons, and Tad must have a few more shorts."

A sudden thought burst into my mind. "Mrs. Wilson, you wouldn't know someone named Rocky, would you? He drives a dirty white car, smallish, sort of—"

A knowing smile spilled across her face. "No," she said. "But I'll keep my eyes open."

I felt my cheeks flush. "If you find out, you'll let me know, won't you?"

Mrs. Wilson nodded. As she went out the door she gave me a conspiratorial wink. It made me feel queer, almost like I'd been caught telling a lie.

It was almost five before I got home. Our dining room's cool haven welcomed me, and I headed straight for the refrigerator. I helped myself to lemonade, and the ice clinked against the knobby blue glass. I rubbed its coolness against my flaming cheeks on the way to my room.

I was unprepared for what I saw next. My bright red bathing suit lay in the windowsill. *Put something red in your window. I'll see it. I'll know.* I snatched it to the floor.

Then I raced to the porch where Mother was reading. "Who put my bathing suit in the window?" I shouted.

Mother didn't even look up. "Why, I did, Dear. It was wet and dripping all over your rug."

"You had no right to be in my room!"

Mother looked up this time. "I have every right to be in your room," she said quietly.

"Well, if you had to pick it up, why didn't you put it on the clothesline?"

"Melissa, I don't understand you at all. Why should you get so upset over my hanging your bathing suit in the window? You'd think I'd committed a federal offense!"

"Well—" I floundered. "It looks terrible to the neighbors—it's embarrassing!"

I turned away, feeling suddenly ashamed. I stopped beside the telephone on my way back to my room and stared at it. It was ominously quiet, like a solemn black monster biding its time.

I shivered. "Scattered thunder showers," I whispered. I wondered what time my own private storm of fear would break.

8 / Melissa's Psalm

I woke suddenly. One moment I'd been wading in a sun-dappled pool searching for some unknown lost thing, the next I was lying in my room staring at the green bedspread making its own precarious mountain over my feet.

A dream-like haze spread a thin mist of anxiety over me. Like an elusive shadow it shifted and moved away. I turned restlessly, struggling to grasp it. But it eluded me like a wayward butterfly fluttering just out of reach.

I shivered. Big drops rustled the leaves of the vine maple outside my window. I got out of bed and padded over to it. A cool breeze wafted across my bare shoulders. Goose pimples erupted on my legs. I stood there, breathing deep gulps of the cleansed air with its peculiar sweetness of damp dust and freshened grass and leaves.

A car horn tooted. Quickly I shut the window and ran to my bed, snuggling my warm blanket beneath my chin.

I shut my eyes tightly. Colleen's laughing face, a swinging sand bucket, something gold glinting in the sun, encircling Darryl's head—one followed the other in rapid succession through my head, bobbing like floating pictures. Then there was Chris, so gentle, so eager to help. His brown eyes had that laughing, come-hither look someone had caught in the photo I cared for so tenderly. That was it! I'd think about Chris! But Chris's face faded and instead I saw an ugly flattened one. A bright red flag fluttered over his head.

That was it! The hidden anxiety that had been lurking so near! My red bathing suit had signaled a false message. I've heard from Colleen, it had shouted. I know where she is!

"Oh, Lord," I whispered, "if it's all the same to you, I'd just as soon he hadn't seen that bright red. But if he did, Lord, what shall I do?"

I lay very still. Something deep inside me whispered, *My Word is truth.*

"Truth," I said, and I said it right out loud. "I'll just have to tell him the truth about my bathing suit, no matter how dumb it sounds."

A curious calm spread itself over my troubled thoughts. I reached for my Bible and turned to the Psalms.

I read Psalm 70 through once, slowly, thoughtfully. Then again, in growing amazement. Why, this was my innermost feelings put into words! Slowly I read it again, only this time I spoke it to God in my own words.

"Rescue me, Oh my God. Lord, please hurry to help me. That creature of the night, Lord, he's my enemy. He may even be after my life. He seems to delight in hurting me. Confuse him! Shame him! Don't let him keep mocking me!

"Lord, I'm your follower. Fill me with joy, the joy that can only come when Colleen is safe home. Let all those in my family who love you dearly exclaim, 'What a wonderful God you are!'

"But I'm in deep trouble. Hurry to help me, for only you know where my sister is. Only you can save me from the creature of the night. Oh, Lord don't delay. Hurry!"

Before I put my Bible down I carefully wrote in my own private title: *Melissa's Psalm, A Cry for Help.* Then I added the date.

In the morning there was a quick rap on my door. "Melissa!" Mother's voice called. My heart gave a sudden leap. Could it be the telephone? But Mother just wanted me to run to the store for some margarine.

I got out of bed and reluctantly opened my closet. Today didn't seem like a jeans day. I chose, instead, a pair of dark-green corduroy slacks and a leafy pale-green blouse. When I was dressed, I felt feminine and cool—almost too cool. I'd need a sweater once I got outside. But none of my sweaters complemented my outfit. Then I thought of Colleen's green and rust sweater-jacket. It would be just the thing! I left my own sweaters heaped on my bed and hurried to Colleen's room.

At her closed door, I hesitated. It wasn't that Colleen would care if I borrowed her sweater—we often wore each other's clothes. It was the memory of that gashed and blood-stained mirror that stayed my hands and made me dread opening the door.

I took a deep breath and shoved it open. The bedspread was arranged neatly again on the bed, the bureau drawers tightly closed, the pictures straightened. The utter neatness shouted *Mother!* Only the white pillowcase carefully taped over the broken mirror hinted anything unusual. *It's like a sheeted corpse*, I thought, and hated myself for such morbid imaginings.

Deliberately, I turned my back and opened Colleen's sweater drawer. White, cream, shades of blue, but no rust and green. Then I opened her closet door and carefully pushed the hangers apart, but there was no sweater there either. "But it's her favorite," I whispered. I knew it had been there the night I'd slept in her room. I remembered it plainly, lumped in a heap on her dressing table.

I hurried into the kitchen. "Mother, I can't find Colleen's sweater—the rust and green one. Did you put it somewhere?"

Mother put the milk pitcher on the table. "No, Dear. It wasn't in her room when I cleaned it up."

"But it was there before—before—"

"Colleen has so many clothes. I don't know how you can tell if it was or not. Will you please get the margarine?"

"But it *was*," I insisted.

"Well, it's not there now. And there's no use looking in the wash, either. It isn't there."

I turned away helplessly, but I wasn't alone. Gabriel's cold nose snuggled into my hand. An idea leaped into my mind.

"Come on, Gabriel."

Together we hurried into Colleen's room again. I opened the sweater drawer. "Smell, Gabriel. Smell."

Gabriel sniffed obediently, his dark eyes shining, his eager little tail trembling.

"Find her, Gabriel. Help me find her."

I think he understood, for he poked his head into the closet and sniffed her shoes. Then he leaped on her bed, smelling the bedspread, the pillow, his tail a big question mark. I carried a blouse over to him and let him sniff it.

"Smell, Gabriel. It's Colleen. Find her for me, please. Find her!" His tail wagged gently, and he thrust his nose reassuringly into my hand.

"Melissa, I need that margarine!"

"Coming!" I yelled.

It didn't take long to get the margarine. When I came back, Mother was sitting at the table stirring her coffee, her cat-just-swallowed-the-canary look radiating from her. I looked at her curiously as I plunked the margarine onto a saucer.

"Well?" I asked.

"I had a telephone call while you were gone." My heart

lurched. "Guess who?"

I swallowed hard. "I wouldn't know."

"Star Flower's mother. We're going to lunch together."

"Oh, Mother!" I felt like hugging her. "How did you ever get acquainted?"

Mother sipped her coffee, the purring look still in her eyes. "I made it a point to be friendly every time I was over at the Food King—You told me she worked there. Anyway, I told her all about you and how "taken" you were with Star Flower—"

"Leila," I corrected.

"Yes, I know. Anyway, it surprised me the way she seemed to take to me, her being quite a bit younger than I. Well, to make a long story short, I asked her to call me someday when she was free and we'd have lunch together. We're going out to the Silver Leaf today."

"What about Darryl?"

"He's lots better. If you'll just keep him inside and quiet."

I sighed. "Of course. Just as long as his temperature doesn't sky-rocket again. If he started talking crazy, it'd scare me."

"Kids are funny. They can be so sick and then just pop right out of it. Anyway, if you'd just pray that somehow—"

I nodded. Right then one of my greatest desires was that Star Flower would begin to talk.

I thought about it while I straightened the living room—books in the bookcase, newspapers folded by the fireplace.

Darryl was observing me. "Melissa, if you had two wishes, what would you wish for?"

"That Colleen be found, of course. And that Star Flower would be able to talk."

"Why can't she talk?" Darryl wanted to know.

"We don't know. That's why Mother went to lunch with her mother." I dropped the books in a heap beside the couch and took Darryl's hands in mine. "Darryl, let's turn my wishes into prayers."

And so we did. Darryl was blunt and to the point. "Lord, please send Colleen home. Do it in a hurry. And please help that little girl learn how to talk. Amen." He looked up. "Well, do you think He heard us?"

"Why, Darryl! Of course He did. The Bible says He does."

"What if He says, 'No?'"

I stared down at him. His eyes were big and blue and full of unspoken questions. "Well," I said slowly, "I guess we'd just have to accept it. But—" I leaped to my feet. "I'm not going to believe the answer is no—not yet, anyway."

The morning dragged on. I wandered aimlessly from room to room, picking up a book, putting it down, rearranging the mantel, replacing my sweaters in their drawers. Darryl was asleep, and I was fooling around with my macrame when the telephone rang.

I had the phone in my hand before it could ring the second time.

"Melissa—"

Fear made a funny taste in my mouth. "Yes?"

"You have something to tell me?"

Truth, I thought, *just truth*. "Well—" I blurted. "I know what you're thinking, but—well—that red thing in the window—it was my bathing suit drying. Mother picked it up off the floor and put it there without my knowing—"

"Your bathing suit?" Sarcasm and disbelief dripped from his voice.

"We did have a phone call. My little brother thought it was from Colleen but we don't know. She hung up or was disconnected or something."

Excitement tinged his voice. "Did you find out where it was from?"

"No." A horrid feeling settled deep inside. "We don't even know for sure if it was Col—"

"Listen, kid. I've had enough of your covering for your sister. Now, did you, or did you not, hear from her?"

"We thought it was her, but we don't know. We were disconnected."

"And when was this?"

"Yesterday—I mean last night."

"Kid, just what do you mean?"

Sudden confidence and anger spurted into me. "Listen, Rocky. I really don't have to tell you anything. Colleen is MY sister and her disappearance has nothing to do with you or YOUR affairs!"

There was a startled silence, then, "How did you know my name?"

"Never mind how I know your name! Maybe, just maybe, I know more about you than you think!"

Another silence, and then—a click.

As I slammed the receiver down I wondered if I'd said the wrong thing. I looked around for reassurance from Gabriel but he was nowhere to be seen. I went out the door and called, but he didn't appear.

I went into my bedroom and resolutely pulled out Colleen's diary. *It's now or never,* I thought. Quickly I skimmed over the pages. No Rocky leaped out at me; only George and Paul and Jim and Dale and Joe. I drew a deep breath of relief and shoved it under my mattress.

The phone rang again and I ran back to the living room. "Melissa, it's me, Chris."

Relief gladdened my voice. "Oh, Chris. At first I thought—I thought—"

"What did you think?"

"I thought it might be my anonymous telephone-caller."

"Did he call again?"

"Just a few minutes ago. And Chris, when I called him *Rocky,* he got really upset!"

"That's it!" he cried. "If we could just find out who Rocky is, I dare say our mystery might be solved."

"Really?" I asked dubiously.

"What else did he say?"

"Nothing much. Maybe I was wrong, but I did tell him about that strange telephone call in the middle of the night. He thought I knew more than I was telling—so I got mad."

"Melissa, that guy worries me. I still think you should tell your folks."

"No," I said, "not yet. Chris, I forgot to tell you earlier—I did ask Darryl if he'd taken that sand bucket. He said he hadn't—"

Chris' voice changed. "I wasn't calling about mysterious phone calls and sand buckets. It's about the youth banquet. Melissa, will you go with me?"

"With you? Oh, Chris, I'd love it!"

"Okay, that's settled. Let me know what color your dress will be. All right? I'll call you tonight."

I sat there a long time after Chris hung up. And I wasn't thinking of sand buckets or disappearing sisters. I was thinking about a dress, a very special dress, that would turn plain ordinary me into somebody special.

9 / The Pink Dress

I wandered into my room and opened the closet. I took my dresses out one by one and looked at them critically. The red and white checked one was too small. The white with the blue roses was nice, but I'd worn it to church too many times. The yellow with the scattered tiny bouquets of flowers was last year's favorite.

I held it up against my reflection in the mirror. It seemed to make my complexion turn sallow. My face even seemed to grow long and thin. I tossed the dress aside.

I sat cross-legged on the bed and thought. Perhaps Dad would give me the money for a new one—or the material for one. I remembered the pale lilac dress Pam had made just before school was out. It had turned out beautifully. Maybe, just maybe. . . .

I fell into a daydream. A dress, a silky green dress rippled to my feet. In it I moved with fluid grace. And my eyes! No longer ordinary gray, they shone with green lights. And Chris was looking at me in admiration.

"Lord," I murmured, "if you could help me find a dress. It doesn't have to be green exactly—or silky. It just needs to be special—so very, very special."

I pushed my daydreaming thoughts aside and went back to my responsibility tucked away on the couch. If only he would stay asleep! But of course he didn't.

When Mother came home she was all bubbly and distracted, enthusiastically hunting telephone numbers and setting up appointments. It had been hard to talk to her about a new dress. But I knew I should have been glad. Leila's mother had been so eager to find help. And Mom, well Mom was like that, needing something to do for somebody else.

I hadn't really felt like talking much anyway. Darryl had wakened full of energy. He should have been outside playing cowboys and Indians instead of cooped up in a book-haunted house. I'd had a terrible afternoon keeping him entertained and reasonably contained.

My voice had risen, climbing higher and higher until Darryl had complained, "Your voice is like an auctioneer! Do this! Do that! Go here! Ugh!"

Well, I hadn't liked it any better than he had. And he needn't think I did either.

I could hear something at the front door now. Pushing, scratching, and then a whine. Gabriel! I'd been so preoccupied that I'd forgotten he'd disappeared! I dashed through the living room and flung open the door.

He stood there, tail wagging, eyes gleaming with pride. Between his teeth was Colleen's green and rust sweater!

"Gabriel! Where did you get this? How did you find it!"

His tail moved faster, his front paws beating a joyful dance on the steps. I picked the sweater up then knelt beside my angel.

"Good boy, Gabriel. Good boy." I smoothed the soft white hair between his eyes. They were full of adoration. I put my face next to his and crooned silly love words that didn't mean anything, except everything.

"Gabriel," I whispered, "where did you find it? Oh, if only you could talk! If only you could find Colleen!"

His little nose made dabbing motions on my face. As I held his eager body close I knew beyond a shadow of a doubt that he would find Colleen if he could.

I tried to tell Mother that. But my excitement was instantly doused. Mother turned to Darryl.

"What were you doing, taking Colleen's good sweater outside and leaving it. Don't you know sweaters cost money?"

I felt sorry for him later. I was almost asleep when he came into my room, a miserable, repentant figure silhouetted against the window.

He just stood there breathing hard and snuffling every few breaths. I opened the covers wide. "Come on in, Darryl."

In one big leap he was snuggled against me. The snuffling sounds turned to sobs and I held him close, my angry feelings evaporating into the night.

At last he was still. I smoothed his hair gently, then asked, "Aren't you going to tell me what's wrong?"

He was at it again—big hiccupping sobs that came from deep within. At last the words came, slowly, hesitantly, achingly. "Nobody—loves—me. Nobody—"

"Darryl," I reassured him, "I love you. It's just that you've been sick and getting on everyone's nerves because you couldn't play outside. We all love you."

"Mother—thinks—I'm a liar. But I'm not—I never was in Colleen's room."

I patted his shoulder clumsily. "I know you weren't, Darryl. And I don't think Mother really thought so either. She was just upset."

He seemed to take comfort from my words for the sobbing and hiccupping stopped. My heart went out to him. I wished Mother were more understanding.

I pulled him closer. I knew how he felt. Maybe Mother didn't exactly take me for a liar but she sure played down everything I came up with. Tonight had had a very flattening effect.

I looked out the window. The stars were splendorous. One seemed to wink with a blue light, another with a dash of red. I pointed it out to Darryl and he was instantly distracted, his imagination stirred. Together we gazed at the Milky Way.

And then, with the glowing combination of starlight and street light and moonlight trembling on the telephone lines, my eyes grew heavy. I had found there was something definitely comforting and reassuring about a soft little flannelled person cuddling you close and looking to you for answers.

"Melissa." It was a soft whisper heavy with sleep. "I'm going to tell you a secret someday. I didn't hide Colleen's sweater but I did hide something else."

"What—"

"I buried it though. Gabriel won't find it." His voice was growing heavy.

"Go to sleep," I mumbled. "We'll talk about it in the morning."

But we didn't. There were too many other things to do. First, there was the question of the dress. Elaine phoned early, bubbling and excited. Chris had called her and asked if she would go with his friend, Steve, to the banquet.

I felt like hugging myself when I hung up the telephone. And I did. I even danced around the room a little bit. Why, with a terrific speaker, three youth groups combining into one wonderful banquet—anything could happen.

Elaine needed Jesus. Sometimes I felt she was close, so very close. Perhaps the banquet would be the deciding factor.

Mother was more cheerful this morning and Dad promised I

could have a new dress. My little world felt full and happy.

"May Elaine and I go to town today and look?" I asked.

Mother smiled. "You'd better do more than look," she said. "If you should decide to sew it, you'll have to get the pattern and everything you'll need right away. Is Elaine getting a new dress too?"

I nodded. "She's going to make hers. She's a terrific seamstress, I guess. She makes all her own clothes and Leila's too."

Elaine, Leila and I toured the shops in search of that special dress for each of us. Or, rather, it was I who pushed aside dress after dress, and carried innumerable ones into the dressing rooms. Elaine haunted the long counters of materials, fingering the fabrics, holding them up to the light, shaking her head over some and nodding over others.

In the end we both came out clutching fabrics and patterns. Elaine was elated; I was doubtful and uneasy; Leila proudly possessed each of our free hands. Her sparkling eyes and joyous floating steps did something to me inside.

"Tomorrow is her appointment," I said.

I wished I hadn't mentioned it. Elaine's face wilted. Fear passed over her features. She looked down at her sister. "Will you come?" she asked.

"Of course," I promised. I almost wished I hadn't, as an icy foreboding dipped into my stomach. If something was terribly wrong, what word of comfort would I have?

A flash of pink in the window across the street beckoned to me. "Look!" I cried. "We haven't been to that store yet and I see dresses in the window."

"Silly," Elaine protested, "we've already bought material. We're committed now."

"It doesn't cost to look," I said gayly. So we crossed the street. And there it was in the window, the most lovely dress I'd ever seen. True, it wasn't the green dress of my dreams, but there was something about it. I just stopped and stared.

It was the most lovely shade of pink! The neckline was scooped and the lines were simple. The sleeves flared out and fell to the wrist. It was the way the fabric flowed, gently molding the mannequin's figure that set it apart. I knew I had to try it on.

"Don't be foolish," Elaine protested. "Have you looked at the price tag?"

"I don't care. And since I can't buy it anyway the price doesn't matter does it?"

I stepped into the shop and asked the saleslady if they had the dress in my size. She brought it to me and led the way to the dressing room.

As I slipped the delicious pink creation over my head, it settled in soft folds to the floor. I looked at myself in the mirror.

It did all I had dreamed it would, and more. Somehow my eyes seemed more expressive and luminous, my lips more softly curved. Even my skin took on a clearness it hadn't had before. I could even visualize Colleen's amethyst nestled in the hollow at my throat. It would have been so perfect!

I opened the fitting room door. "It's beautiful," Elaine breathed.

Leila reached out and touched the dress. Her lips moved, puckering in a p.

"Pretty!" I said loudly. "Pretty!"

"Pretty," she whispered.

"Did you hear her?" Elaine cried.

My heart was too full to answer. Both Elaine and I knelt down and took her in our arms. It was a three-cornered hug if I ever saw one. And then laughing we made it into a three-cornered kiss too. It was a perfect moment and Leila loved it. Her dark eyes shone like stars and the minute she was free she whispered it again and again, "Pretty, pretty."

"I don't understand it," Elaine kept repeating, "I just don't understand it."

"I don't either. Unless—"

"Unless what?"

"It's the beginning of an answer to prayer."

We were silent then. Softly I fingered the pink fabric. I hated to take it off. Leila's whispered word had made it more precious than before.

It was hard to leave the dress with the helpful saleslady and face the door. We took the bus, and then I made it a point to walk home with Elaine and Leila.

I'd never been there before, since we always met in the park. But today I wanted to understand these sisters more. I wanted to share their lives in a new way. I was startled when Elaine stopped beside a battered, gray gate.

"This is where we live," she said awkwardly.

I stared. It wasn't at all the way I'd imagined it would be. It was an older, two-story house with peeling gray paint, set back from the street by an expanse of unkempt lawn. It had a barren, almost unlived-in look, though there was a bicycle parked at the front door and shades drawn at the windows.

"We haven't been here long enough to fix it up much," Elaine explained.

"But think of what you could do!" I rattled nervously. "Why, with petunias and marigolds along the path and a sandbox under the tree for Leila—and roses on the fence—"

Elaine's feet shifted. I could tell she didn't want to ask me in. I knelt for Leila's good-bye hug. Her dark eyes were dewy and her arms seemed to cling more tightly than ever.

I looked back once. The house regarded me without expression, its drawn shades almost like sullen, closed eyelids. Why had I thought it had no personality? I turned away.

A rock skidded on the ground close to my feet. And then another. Quickly I turned, but there was no movement. The house and street were silent, brooding. I ran towards home.

I told Mom all about my outing as I spread the material on the dining room table. The fabric lay in a lovely heap reminding me of the clumps of autumn crocuses that bloomed in our yard in September.

Mother looked at it more closely. "Why, it's beautiful," she murmured. "I like the way the white thread runs through it."

"Like autumn crocus?"

"Like *what*?"

"Nothing," I said. I pulled out the flowered trim Elaine and I had chosen. "See? We'll trim the neck and sleeves with this."

She wrapped it thoughtfully around her fingers. "It's going to be lovely," she said, a faraway look gathering in her eyes. I knew she wasn't really thinking about the dress.

I gathered up the material and stuffed it into the bag. "Mother, I wish you could have seen the dress at Nordstrom's. It was the most lovely pink, and when I tried it on, I knew it was the perfect dress."

"Then why—"

"I'd already bought the lavender. And besides, the price was atrocious. Mother, why do you think Leila just now said her first word? It was so wonderful! And then, when I walked them home, it all sort of faded. I think Elaine is ashamed of her house. It's so—oh, I don't know—faded and unloved, maybe. I knew she didn't want me to come in."

Mother nodded. "People feel like that sometimes. I remember

when I was a teenager, how I hated our house always being so cluttered. And yet Mom tried—I know she did; but there were six of us."

The telephone rang. It was Mary Wilson. My heart did a double flip. I didn't want to baby-sit!

But she hadn't called about baby-sitting at all. "About that Rocky—well—Umm. I think I've found him for you. He's dark—good-looking, umm—rugged—"

"Where does he live?" I asked breathlessly.

"It's on that off-beat corner on Avery Drive. A faded gray house that's back from the street a bit."

My heart did another flip. Elaine's house! But it couldn't be. Her brother's name wasn't Rocky, it was Joe. *Maybe it's Joe's friend—or maybe it's Joe's nickname,* another voice seemed to whisper.

"Honey, are you still there?"

"Yes—I was just thinking. I think I know which house it is. Goodness, Mrs. Wilson, I sure appreciate your calling. How did you find out?"

Her laugh was low and amused. "Just kept my ears open, Honey. Just kept my ears open. Anyway, good luck."

I expect I'll need it, I thought as I put the receiver down. Why, if Rocky were Joe, and Mother was trying to help Leila, and I was trying to win Elaine to Christ, the wrong word or even suspicion could blast everything we were trying to do into a million pieces. I'd just have to put Mrs. Wilson's telephone call out of my mind if I could, and concentrate instead on making my dress for the banquet. The thought made a warm rosy glow go through me.

It made me think of a pink dress, a lovely pink dress that could now be only part of a precious memory; a little girl's glowing face shining up at me, a little voice whispering huskily, "Pretty, pretty," and little fingers caressing pink softness.

A beautiful pink dress—blessed memory. "Dear Lord . . . I thank you."

10 / The Unexpected Happens

"You'll have to vacuum before you leave," Mother said. I stood there in my brown cords with brown and red flowered blouse and stared at her. "I told you last night it had to be done before you left this morning."

"But I'll be late!"

"Not really. Not if you get at it right away. You're early."

It was true. I had planned it that way. I wanted that extra time with Elaine so we could plan the pattern layout. But there wasn't any use discussing it with Mother. She'd told me about the vacuuming the night before and I had forgotten.

I tossed my purse in the chair and headed for the closet. The vacuum and hoses flopped out. In a few minutes it was roaring— but not for long. The "check bag" button popped up. ·

Irritated, I turned it off and opened the lid. The bag was out with a twist of my fingers. But there was something wrong. I was sure I heard a strange hum coming from it.

I lifted it to my ear and then let out a yell. A bee was crawling on my fingers. I dropped the bag on the floor. Another bee was coming out, and another and another and another! I raced over to the window and tugged at it. A sting on the side of my neck made me push harder. Stubbornly it resisted, then finally slid open. I grabbed the bag and flung it out the window, but not before another bee had stung my arm!

"What on earth—" Mother was standing in the doorway.

"Don't come in" I yelled. "There're more buzzing around!" I slammed the door shut behind me and leaned against it. "They came out of the vacuum bag," I explained.

A funny, calculating look came into Mother's eyes. "I wonder—Darryl was vacuuming the window ledges outside." She turned and disappeared.

I went into the kitchen and made a baking soda paste to put on my stings. They were already hot and swelling—the paste felt cool.

82

Then I went in search of the insect spray. I found it at last on a high shelf in the basement. After I sprayed the room I looked at myself in the mirror. My neat blouse was rumpled. There were white dust streaks on the collar and I smelled distinctly of bug spray. I looked at my clock. I was too late for my meeting with Elaine.

Worried thoughts tumbled through my mind. Would Elaine think that I didn't want to be her friend because I'd seen her house? Or, that I thought I was too good for her?

At that moment I could have gladly strangled my little brother. But then a picture of Darryl with a vacuum hose, snatching bees out of the air and off of the flowers made me giggle. I would have laughed, if my neck and arm hadn't been so sore.

I went down to the park where we'd promised to meet, then over to the bus stop. But they were gone. I stopped by her house on an odd impulse and stood and looked at it from the corner. It looked the same as yesterday: unloved, secretive, depressing, the blinds still drawn, the door shut.

Back home, I vacuumed up the dead bees. Then I spread my lavender material on the living room rug and contemplated my pattern.

I was on my knees holding the scissors in my hand, trying to work up enough courage to cut, when a shadow fell across it. I looked up. Elaine stood there, her face white, her mouth working in a helpless way I'd never seen before. I leaped to my feet, opening my arms. I could feel her trembling against my body. It reminded me of Star Flower and how I'd held her close.

Words came tumbling out. "Oh, Melissa! She didn't respond to the tests! She may not be able to hear!"

My own world darkened. "Oh, Elaine—"

We went outside and sat together on the porch railing. Sounds I'd seldom paid attention to hammered on my ears with a bittersweet nearness: the neighbor kids shouting, a mother calling, a bee buzzing—

Elaine's voice was a hoarse whisper. "There'll be more tests. she's to see a doctor—"

I hooked my heels behind the bottom rail and stared straight ahead. Thoughts were running through my mind, thoughts I wanted to share but didn't know how.

"Maybe—" I said. Elaine stared at me silently. "Maybe—just maybe—God has a special plan for Leila. I mean—well—God never lets anything in our lives be wasted—not even the hard things. And God loves Leila, I know it. Somehow I think He's going to use this in a wonderful way."

My thoughts raced ahead. I imagined Leila as a young woman—lithe, beautiful, loving. I seemed to see her surrounded by children, to hear her laugh—

I tried to tell Elaine what I was thinking. It seemed to comfort her, although we said little. After awhile we went back into the house.

Elaine looked at the pattern pinned to the material on the floor. Vaguely she picked up my scissors. "Let me help you with this," she said.

"Just a minute." I put my hand on her shoulder. "I really wanted to be with you today. But something happened—"

"It's all right. I know you would have been there if you could." She dropped to her knees, the scissors poised above the lavender.

"Wait!" I cried. "I'm not sure—"

Elaine picked up the pattern directions and studied them carefully. "Why, you did it just right. Do you care if I help?"

Care! As if I cared. Why, I'd been sitting there at least an hour trying to drum up the courage to cut.

I told her that, and she laughed.

Her quick, efficient hands guided the scissors effortlessly as she told me how to mark each piece. When we were finished with that, she showed me how to pin them together and do the stay stitching.

My sewing machine began to hum, and the dress took shape before my eyes. I tried on the bodice and with a few deft motions Elaine made it fit perfectly. Why, it was going to be beautiful! Perhaps not as beautiful as the pink dress, but something special in its own right.

When it was time to leave, Elaine drew me outside. "I'll help you tomorrow," I said awkwardly.

Elaine's smile was tremulous. "You've helped me today, Melissa. More than you'll ever know."

"You are my sister," I said impulsively. "You and Leila are both sisters to me."

Elaine's eyes shone with a sudden intense light. Her hands clung to mine. Then she was gone. I watched her until she disappeared from view.

The next few days fairly flew. Elaine and I spent every spare moment we could find cutting and fitting. My own dress emerged, a shimmering, lavender creation edged with dainty flowers.

Elaine's was navy blue trimmed with delicate white edging. When she put it on, I was amazed. Somehow the navy brought out the blue tones in her hair, the dark luster in her wide, expressive eyes.

Leila's hearing loss turned out to be less than total, and fitted with a hearing aid, she was plunged into the world of sound. The Doctor said she should be placed in a stimulating environment to make up for the time she had lost. He recommended the training center for exceptional children and encouraged Elaine and I to volunteer our help.

I found a new world there. A world of toothless grins and wide eyes behind thick glasses, of deep dimples and sunburned noses. I doled out encouraging hugs, wiped runny noses, cut out pictures and guided uncertain little hands through a multitude of projects.

To my amazement, I found I loved it. It was something I could throw myself into, oddly enough, lose myself. I'd walk out into the bright sunshine after my hours there, and feel I was stepping into a different world.

One morning, Mrs. Miles, the teacher, brought her guitar and the room vibrated with folk tunes. We all held hands and danced—"One step forward, two steps back. Clap your hands and tap, tap, tap."

Leila's moist hand snuggled in mine, her lips parted with excitement. I lifted both our hands in a signal to Elaine across the room and tilted my head towards Leila.

Elaine smiled back, her eyes alive with feeling. *How much she loves her sister* I thought. *Her greatest longing is for Leila's happiness.*

But my joy evaporated later, when I found Leila alone, backed into a corner by the cement wall bordering the playground. Her head was drooped, and though tears marked her cheeks, her face had a wooden look.

"Leila," I whispered, "Leila." I sat down beside her and pulled her close.

A freckled little boy with glasses plunked down beside us. "He tore up her flowers," he said pointing to the ground. He squinted through the medley of whirling arms and legs and bright-colored play clothes. "It was him," he pointed, "over there."

I looked instead at the purple and yellow pansy petals lying bruised and broken against the reddish sawdust. Quickly, I scooped then up and got to my feet. "We'll get more later," I said. But Leila's face remained unresponsive.

"Come on!" I called, grabbing Leila's hand. "Let's play London Bridge!" The children flocked around me and Leila was drawn in, in spite of herself. Gradually her face softened, as she began to lose herself in the silly sing-song lyric.

Mrs. Miles took me aside later. "I was watching you with Leila on the playground," she said. "You handled the situation beautifully."

My mood spiraled upward. "Thank you," I said shyly. "Sometimes adjusting to the world is hard."

"It is," Mrs. Miles agreed. "And Leila is coming into it a little behind the rest. But she'll catch up. I don't think we need to worry if she lingers on the fringes for a while."

I told Elaine about it while we walked home. Then, suddenly, I was struck with the realization that I hadn't thought of Colleen once all morning. It swept over me like a darkness and gave me almost a physical shock. Hurriedly, I mumbled a good-bye to the sisters and rushed home.

Mother was outside with a hoe in her hand, singing the way she used to do over her marigolds and roses. "How can you be so happy when Colleen is—" I demanded.

She was instantly quiet. Then, "Melissa, darling, one has to go on living and trusting. Otherwise something inside will dry up. And our Lord says we're to think on things beautiful, lovely and of good report. And remember, Melissa, He gives songs in the night— when things are dark."

Pain twisted inside me. "Oh, Mother," I cried. I went over and hugged her. "It's just that I was feeling guilty because I'd enjoyed myself so much today at the center. I guess I just didn't understand.

But I was glad Mother had. I went away marveling at her wisdom.

I tried to tell Chris about it down at the tennis courts the day of the banquet. We lay on the grass, our rackets beside us. Overhead the climbing red roses smiled down at us beneath the blue canopy of summer sky. I lay on my stomach, thoughtfully nibbling the tender end of a grass shoot.

"Every time I go to the center, the time flies. Something about it just consumes me. Maybe it's those little kids, the way they're beginning to love me. Maybe—oh, I can't explain it. It just satisfies me somehow. I wish I could be there all day."

Chris looked at me doubtfully. "It must be awful hard on your patience—I mean, the retarded ones. I think it would drive me—"

"Oh, no!" I cried. "You don't understand. It fulfills something deep inside. Just to be able to break into their world means so much!"

Chris was silent, his eyes on some faraway distant place. "What are you thinking?" I blurted.

"I was just wondering," he said, slowly, thoughtfully. "Do you remember how when we were first getting acquainted, we talked a little bit about our future plans? Remember how you said you were just drifting, not really knowing what you wanted?"

"Chris, do you think this might be one way God is saying He wants me to work with handicapped children?"

"I don't know, Melissa. But it might be an indication. What do the instructors down at the center think, or have you talked—"

"I didn't ask, but Mrs. Miles took me aside yesterday and asked me if I knew that I had an unusual talent with the children. It made me feel awfully good—like I'd gotten a promotion or something."

Chris leaped to his feet, pulling me up beside him. We linked hands and did a silly little dance around and around with Gabriel yipping at our heels.

"Oh, Chris, do you suppose—"

"I don't know, but I think it's exciting. How's your little Star Flower doing?"

"She still isn't *saying* anything, Chris. But you should see her respond to music! She loves it! And she's beginning to interact with the others during game time."

Chris was watching me intently. "You really love her, don't you?"

"Chris, I do. I really do."

"I think it's great. How's your relationship with the Lord these days?"

We flopped back on the grass. I took a deep breath. "It's been pretty special. I feel I can talk to Him about anything. I've even been reading about the different women of the Bible and seeing how practical their lives were. Like Dorcas. She didn't have any great talents, particularly, but she did have a needle and thread. And she used them to serve others."

"That's great. And remember, the Bible does say He gives us a desire for the work of our hands."

I thought about it all the way home. The excitment of seeing God's leading in my life was coupled with another excitement. The banquet. Chris would see me really dressed up. I felt a slight pang when I thought of the pink dress, but it didn't last. My lavender was lying on the bed waiting for me to slip into it.

The instant I opened the door, I sensed a spirit of anticipation. Did I bring it with me or was something happening I didn't know about?

Mother came flying out of the kitchen. There was a sparkle in her eyes and a lilt in her voice that I hadn't seen in a long time.

"What's up?" I asked brightly.

Mother smiled. Was there a secret glinting in the corner of her mouth?

"Well?"

"Well? What?"

I grinned. "Do I smell a nice secret or do my senses deceive me?"

Mother just laughed. "Can't a mother be excited about her daughter going to the banquet with the finest Christian boy she knows?"

I felt myself flush a deep pink. "Oh, Mother," I protested. I started towards my room but Mother stopped me. Her hand on my arm was guiding me to the bathroom.

"You'd better shower now. I've put your robe in the bathroom and I've left my own rose soap." She pushed me through the door and shut it firmly behind me.

I stood there feeling foolish, wondering why Mother had suddenly become so overly helpful. It didn't fit together.

But I went ahead and showered; figuring out Mother's odd behavior would have to wait. The water's pounding "fingers" invigorated me, and thoughts of Chris danced in my head.

When I was finished, I wrapped myself in my robe, and wound my towel into a turban on my head. Then I made a dash for my room.

At the doorway I stopped and gasped. The dress lying on the bed wasn't lavender. It was pink—the very dress I'd tried on at Nordstrom's!

And then Elaine and Mother were beside me. "Do you like it?" Mother cried.

"Were you surprised?" Elaine asked.

I walked over, and with trembling fingers caressed the soft pink. "I—I don't know what to say—" I stammered. "How—how did you?"

"Elaine took me into town and showed it to me. She said she was sure she could make a duplicate if I could get her the material. So here it is. Your own special dress, created by Elaine."

"And assisted by your very own mother," Elaine explained. "You won't mind not wearing the lavender, will you?"

"Oh, Elaine! My lavender was all right, but this—Elaine, Mother, how can I ever thank you?"

"By getting out of that dumb robe and modeling it for us!" Elaine laughed.

My hands flew to my towel. "After I've fixed my hair," I protested.

We all laughed. Elaine gave me a quick hug. "I've got to go dress now. I'll be watching for you."

I nodded, my heart too full for words. Mother hugged me too. "Go ahead and dress, Honey. I'll see you when you're ready." At the door she turned. "And, Melissa, I want you to know I've noticed a difference in you. It isn't just that you're getting older. You're beginning to grow in the Lord."

A warm glow that had nothing to do with a pink dress filled me. I struggled for words. "It has something to do with learning to wait."

Mother's eyes filled with questions. A slight frown crinkled her forehead. "Wait?"

I picked up the concordance from my nightstand and handed it to her. "When Colleen disappeared, Chris suggested I study the verses about waiting. I've been doing it."

Mother turned the heavy book in her hands. "And?"

"I think I'm learning a little bit about how to wait—God's way. When we do, we're using our waiting time to learn, to grow—to be available—

"And something else—yesterday, when I was reading about Miriam, something jumped out at me. Mother, as young as she was, she knew something about waiting God's way! When she put Moses' ark in the water, she did it knowing that God was going to somehow take care of her brother."

Mother nodded. "Go on."

"Then she held back expectantly when the princess came.

Why, if it had been me I'd have probably raced out from behind those reeds and snatched my brother from the daughter of the wicked pharaoh. But she didn't! She held back and waited to see how God would take care of the problem."

I took a deep breath. "Now she was ready, ready and available. Moses cried and Miriam saw the love and concern on the princess's face. She stepped forward and asked if she could help provide a nurse for her baby brother. Just think how God worked everything together for good for Miriam and her family!"

Mother shut the door and came over to me. Once again she hugged me close. "I love you, Dear."

After she left, I held the dress beneath my chin and looked in the mirror. It was true. It still did that certain something to my eyes and hair. And it did something else, too. It brought back memories of a little girl's voice whispering, "Pretty, pretty."

But this dress was my very own, made with love especially for me. I hugged it close and whispered, "Thank you, Elaine and Mother. And thank you, Lord.

11 / Broken Pink Dreams

When my hair was blown-dry to its silkiest sheen, I picked up my new dress. With hands that were not quite steady, I slid it over my head.

It settled in silky smoothness over my hips, and gently flared to the floor. I struggled with the zipper and then—I held my breath and looked in the mirror.

It was all I remembered and more. The soft lines set off my figure and the subdued pink illumined my skin and eyes. Even my hair seemed to glow with reflected glory.

Candy pink, I thought, and a sudden memory stabbed me. I had seen that lovely pink sheen before. It had been a winter day at the beach and Colleen and I had watched the sun sink into the sea. Its pink glow was reflected in the sky and ocean and candy tuft clouds. Even a pencil-thin jet trail was pink in that shimmering sky.

"Oh, Colleen!" I'd cried. "If only I could paint it, I'd paint it just like it is right now, all pink and glorious!"

Colleen had only shrugged. "It would all fade before you could finish it."

"But I could remember," I'd protested.

"But memories fade too," she'd said. "Come on! Let's run!"

And run we did. Over the pink sand we made a collection of pink footprints, running towards the water and back again, then into crazy circles, around and around.

I remembered. I knew I would never forget. I turned away from the mirror and stole into Colleen's room. Tonight was my night, but in a way, at least in memory, it was Colleen's too. I wanted to wear her star.

I opened her jewelry box slowly and picked up the folded white envelope at the bottom. Carefully, I opened it and slipped my fingers inside. I gasped as Colleen's missing turquoise necklace tumbled into my hand. Frantically, I searched the envelope again—but no golden star with an amethyst center was there.

Dazed, I touched each piece of jewelry in her box, then ran to her dresser. I pulled open each drawer and ran my fingers along the bottom. But there was nothing—nothing.

First Colleen's sweater, and now her star necklace! "Gabriel," I whispered. "Gabriel." A moist, loving nose thrust into my hand.

"Melissa!" Mother's quick step was in the hall. Hurriedly, I gathered my torn emotions into a semblance of order and pasted on my most joyous smile.

Dad's long, low whistle and Mother's admiring, "Oh, Honey, it's perfect for you—just perfect," rewarded me. Even Darryl's startled, "Wow! You look as pretty as a pink candle!" lifted my spirits.

Feeling a delicious combination of little girl and pink flower, I held my arms out and twirled slowly around. My dress fanned out bell-like and I felt prettier than ever. And that was how Chris found us, all laughing together.

He held a white box out to me. As I lifted the cluster of dainty pink roses to my shoulder, I caught his eye. There was something unusually serious in them and his mouth seemed tremulous. I fought back an almost irresistible urge to touch it.

Instead, I fumbled with the pin. "Here," and Dad's big, sure fingers were helping me.

"They're beautiful—just perfect," I breathed.

"And so are you," Chris said as he took my arm and guided me down the steps and onto the path.

Only it wasn't plain earth I was stepping on. It was a candy-pink cloud. I hoped I wouldn't ever have to come down.

I didn't for a long time. Even the prosaic rolls and butter, chicken, mashed potatoes, peas and salad, didn't bring me down.

I didn't come back to earth until I heard Elaine, across the table from us, say to Steve, "Rocky likes things like that."

I didn't hear what Chris was saying. Instead, I leaned forward. "Who's Rocky?" I demanded in a voice that sounded too loud.

Elaine's startled look met mine. "Oh, Rocky's Joe—you know—my brother. Steve and I were talking about my chain." Her fingers touched the fine gold filigree at her neck. "It doesn't really go with this dress, but Rocky wanted me to wear it."

Before my shocked stare, she pulled a shining gold star with an amethyst center from beneath her collar. I gasped, or at least I hoped that was all I did. My lovely pink cloud evaporated and my feet were on the floor and running. I felt rather than saw the surprised looks on the other's faces. But I didn't care! I had to get out of there!

The blast of fresh air revived me. I stopped and grabbed a low-hanging branch of the tree near the entry.

Chris was soon beside me. "Are you all right?"

"I—I think so."

"What happened—back there?"

"Elaine's necklace, Chris—it belongs to Colleen. Her brother took it."

Chris looked at me incredulously. "Lots of necklaces look alike."

I shook my head. "Colleen's was custom-made. The amethyst is her birthstone. Daddy did it for her graduation."

"Maybe it's Elaine's birthstone, too," Chris said.

"But she said *Rocky* gave it to her—and he's her brother. Remember the letter? You said yourself if we could just find out who Rocky—"

"What we weren't thinking was how common 'Rocky' is around this town! Why, since I've been looking, I've met three!"

"But—but—"

"Don't spoil tonight," Chris pleaded. "Forget about Colleen—for awhile, and—oh, I don't know. Just give God a chance to speak to hearts."

I stared at Chris's face. Behind his head I could see clouds shutting out the sun's rays. And they were pink, pale pink, and there were only broken fragments of them streaming along the horizon.

At that moment, the group inside began singing, "I Have Decided to Follow Jesus." I never hear that song but that something painful, poignant and somehow sweet twists inside me.

At that moment, I made a decision. Tonight was a night to entrust Colleen to the Lord in a new way. It was also the night to pray for Elaine, that she too might decide to follow Jesus.

I put my hand on Chris's arm. "Let's go in."

"Are you ready?"

I think I even smiled at him. *Yes, Chris,* I thought, *I'm ready; ready and available. I want to follow Christ—no matter where He leads.*

I really thought I was ready. All through the guest singer's songs, I prayed for Elaine. I watched her face and forgot about the amethyst star gleaming against its navy blue background.

When the speaker took over, I could tell he spoke Elaine's language. At times she laughed at his humorous remarks. At times her dark eyes glowed with a questioning intentness.

"Asking Jesus into your life is just like opening a door," he said. "He's standing there, waiting to be invited in."

"Maybe you feel funny about the dirt, the sin. You say, 'My heart-house is a mess, Lord. I've tried, but it's no use. I can't keep it clean without help. Won't you come in please, and take control?'

"As soon as you acknowledge your sin and need, and invite Him in—He's there to stay—to clean up your life and make everything new."

"Oh, Holy Spirit," I whispered, "Speak to her heart. Make her see how much she needs you."

It was all I could do to keep my eyes tightly shut when the speaker asked for a show of hands of those who wanted to decide for Jesus. Would Elaine raise hers?

Afterwards, Elaine was one of the first to move forward. I tried to see, but it was no use. There were so many up there.

"Oh, Chris," I cried, "do you think Elaine—"

The pressure of his hand on mine was his only answer. But somehow, I felt I knew what his thoughts were.

We were outside then, the night hanging its canopy of stars over us. I lifted my face to them and the warm evening breeze. Eager, excited voices around me lifted me from the ordinary into a different realm. A sense of God's perfection and guidance was all around me.

Then, a hand tugged mine. Elaine stood there, her face shining with something I'd never seen before.

"Elaine! Did you do it?"

"Yes! Yes!" she cried and threw her arms around me. "Oh, thank you, thank you, Melissa! If I had never met you it would never have happened!"

A big blob of feeling welled up into my throat. I swallowed noisily. "Now we're more than sisters," I exclaimed. "We're sisters in Christ!"

Elaine was suddenly distracted. She gestured across the street. "That's my brother's car over there. I wonder—" She grabbed my hand. "Melissa, I want you to meet him. Steve, Chris, you too."

Reluctantly, I looked in the direction she pointed. I recognized the car. Its dirty white sides hung low to the ground and the dark head inside was more than familiar. I was scared.

I didn't want to go over there! But Elaine was pulling me, and Chris was staring at me with a look I couldn't discern.

As we drew close I was instantly conscious of a pair of dark eyes singling me out. They bored into me, shifted to Elaine's necklace and then back to me. I panicked as they taunted me with a secret message only I could interpret: "Tell *her* and you'll be dead!"

I must have acknowledged the introduction. At least for Elaine's sake, I truly hope I did. But the unspoken message was too much for the tender state of my nerves.

I forgot about building bridges of friendship, forgot about strengthening Elaine's new faith, of my determination to follow Jesus. Instead of reaching out, and forgetting myself, I turned inward and let fear have its way. I watched Chris and Steve reach out and shake Rocky's hand, while I stood like a wooden doll with my arms immobile.

I scarcely spoke to either Chris or Steve on the way back to the church. A part of me heard Chris say to Elaine, "Do you suppose he's lonely? I mean to come down, and just stop and watch. He didn't want you for something special did he?"

Elaine's reply seemed to come from faraway. "No, he doesn't have any friends—except Kurt. And somehow I don't think he's a real one. You know, I do think he came just because he was lonely."

The young people were gathering beneath the trees for an outdoor sing and praise time. But I had no heart for it. I'd failed in my new determination to follow Jesus. I wasn't ready and available like I'd thought I was. I slipped away and went alone to the car.

Once inside I bowed my head. "Oh, God," I said, and all my horrid feelings came out in tangled jerks. "I'm sorry—I should have been nice to Joe—but I couldn't. Oh, God—I know that voice on the phone was Joe—I couldn't just push *that* aside. I know I hurt Elaine—but I didn't mean to. And Chris—Oh, God—Chris thinks I'm awful—and I am—but it's awful he has to think it!"

The singing grew unexpectedly louder. I looked up as Chris slid behind the wheel. I gulped hard and sat very still. The singing was instantly softer as he shut the door.

His hand reached out and touched the back of my head. "Well?"

"I'm sorry, Chris," I blurted. "I didn't mean to act so cold toward Elaine's brother. I really didn't."

I could feel his knuckles moving gently back and forth, back and forth, over my hair. It made me feel like crying. But I didn't.

His answer was slow in coming. I could sense an atmosphere of deep disappointment. It covered him like a blanket. "It's just that, well, Elaine's brother seemed so needy, Melissa."

"But how—"

"I don't think he has any friends. And if we could just be his friends we might someday introduce him to Jesus, our greatest friend."

"Are you saying, because I wasn't friendly he might never want to be friends with Jesus? Chris, do you honestly expect me to be friendly just like that—when I recognized his voice!"

"But, Melissa, you can't know that. Voices sound different on the telephone."

"But he jumped through the window into my room!"

"But you said he had a nylon pulled over his face. No one could recognize him that way. And it's been awhile—you may not have remembered him accurately."

"But I know his eyes!" I cried. And then I was silent. Had I been mistaken? For the first time, doubt clawed at me. Were the things that had happened over the past weeks merely figments of an imagination stretched to the breaking point because of my sister's disappearance?

I turned to Chris. "I think I'd like to go home—if it's all right with you."

Instantly he turned the key and the motor rumbled to life. The real me inside felt cold, frozen, dead.

We were silent on the drive home. At the door, Chris gently touched the tip of my chin. "Buck up, girl," he said lightly. And he was gone. I watched him until he got into his car and drove away.

Slowly I opened the door, hoping no one was up. No one was. The house was silent as I slid unnoticed to my room.

The wide expanse of green bedspread seemed to beckon me. For an instant I longed for nothing more than to fall headlong across it and burst into tears. But I wouldn't. Instead of becoming a helpless, frozen blob, I would go out. I would walk and walk and walk, and talk and talk and talk to God, and maybe I would get my feelings sorted out.

I wriggled out of my dress, watching as it fell to the floor in a glorious pink heap. "Broken pink dreams," I whispered. When I tore out of my room dressed in jeans and plaid shirt, I didn't even 'look back.

For a long time I didn't see the night glory, didn't feel its gentle arms enfolding me in its soft darkness. I walked instead through a blur of tears wondering how everything could have gone so wrong.

Into my mind rose a picture of Elijah sitting beneath a juniper tree. His elbows were propped on bent knees spread wide, his mantled shoulders hunched low with discouragement. The blue sky stretched as far as the eye could see—but Elijah wasn't looking. He was all alone and he wanted to die.

At last I looked up at the sky. A pale sickle moon hung there, a transluscent jet trail crossing its slender radiance. The stars toward Portland were pale and anemic, dimmed by light. I turned south where stars, brilliant and unchanging, winked at me.

Suddenly, I sat down on the edge of the graveled country road I'd wandered onto and tried to let some of those stars' bigness enter into me. But it was no use.

My fingers touched the hard road gravel, and then some living, growing thing. I broke its stem and peered at it in the pale moonlight. *Ah,* I thought, *it's that pinkish-white flower that grows on roadsides. It's tough; tough and strong to grow in such a hard, gravelly, busy place.*

I knew then that I wanted to live a long time. I wanted to grow tough and strong. I wanted to see other nights like this, press other flowers between my fingers. And I wanted something else. I really did. I wanted to entrust Chris and Colleen into God's hands in a more real way than I'd ever done before.

I bowed my head. "Lord, forgive me for the mess I made of tonight. Help me to grow strong, even when I hurt; to always be ready and available to people with needs. Oh, Lord, toughen me up. And help me not to be scared of Joe."

"And Elaine—Oh, Lord, I thank you she's a *real* sister now. Help me to be a helping sister—and Chris—and Colleen—" A big lump came into my throat and I couldn't say anything more. But I knew He understood.

Back in my room my crumpled pink dress no longer taunted me. I picked it up and tenderly smoothed its folds. Gently I removed the wilted pink roses. Their faint, elusive fragrance reminded me of something tender, now faraway. But it didn't matter. I even smiled as I pinned them on the wall. No more broken pink dreams for me! I had a Lord whose specialty was fixing broken lives. I leaped into bed and was asleep almost instantly.

12 / The Fair

I must have been asleep for quite awhile, for when I wakened suddenly, the room had that feel of midnight. I lay still trying to grab hold of my dream. It had somehow seemed very important. But the more I tried, the more it slid away from me—like sand running through my fingers, like a goldfish eluding my touch. Frustration started nibbling at me. If only I could pull the dream closer so the importance would come through.

In the dream Darryl had been walking carefully along the top of a white picket fence, balancing a bucket of sand. I could see his lips moving but I wasn't close enough to hear what he was saying. I kept trying to move forward but something was holding me back.

"Darryl!" I'd called, "Darryl!" But he wouldn't even look at me. Then unexpectedly I was free and running towards him. Just as I reached him he tipped the bucket upside down over his head. Instead of sand, a bunch of gold things the size of silver dollars rained down. He said something to me about a secret, and I remembered a feeling of intense excitement welling up inside me. Then he'd made another remark, but I couldn't remember what it was, only that it was somehow very important.

I sat up in bed and flung off my covers. I walked barefoot over to the window and looked out. The sickle moon was gone and the night wasn't as bright as it had been earlier when I'd tramped into the country. The fence outside my window glinted. Quite suddenly, I knew what Darryl had said in my dream. "Buckets and beaches, they do go together."

I felt like laughing, it sounded so silly. I wondered why it had seemed so important. I went back to bed, the blankets warm and comforting. I fell asleep almost at once.

The next week suddenly changed pace and dragged by. Partly because I had to baby-sit the Wilson kids, partly because I missed being at the center with Leila and Elaine, but mostly because Chris didn't call. Even at church he was aloof—at least I thought he was.

I kept busy, trying to keep my mind off things that only hurt and confused me. I threw all my imagination and talents into baby-sitting Tad and Judith. To my surprise, I found they no longer bored me.

I hauled them both to the library and brought back armloads of books. Tad and I spent hours slowly turning pages. "See," I'd say, "car, tree, flower." "Car," he'd imitate, "twee, fower."

I also brought back records of children's songs. Tad laughed and tried to sing with them. Sometimes we clapped and pranced around the room together while Judith cooed in fascinated satisfaction from the playpen.

Tad and I did other things too. We pasted pictures in a scrapbook and built tall towers. I bought him crayons and it was fun to watch him learn to grasp them and make his first uncertain scribbles.

Elaine came over one evening and we had a long talk. I think I'll always remember the sweetness of her crooked smile as I tried haltingly to explain my odd behavior the night of the banquet.

"It's all right, Melissa," she said over and over. "You don't need to explain. I understood that something was bothering you and that you weren't yourself. You don't need to talk about it if you don't want to."

"But Joe must think I'm awful," I said lamely.

"Oh, no," Elaine protested, "I don't think he even noticed. In fact, afterwards he asked a lot of questions about you."

"Like what?"

"Oh, how long had we been friends, what kind of person were you—you know—Were you the loyal sort or just a fair-weather kind." She laughed. "Of course, I told him you were the best friend I'd ever had. I think it surprised him."

"Why?"

"Probably because I'd never had a close friend before." She smiled. "Did you think he was kind of cute?"

"Um—" I mumbled, and quickly changed the subject. We began to talk of other things. But I thought about it a lot. And I wondered.

But I had other things to think of too. More important things. Chris still hadn't called and I could feel my insides beginning to hurt again.

I even confided my feelings to Elaine later that day.

"Want to go see him?" she asked.

"Oh, I couldn't," I muttered. "Anyway I did see him in church Sunday. Be we didn't talk."

"I didn't mean that," she explained. She jumped to her feet. "Come on," she said, "I know where he is right now."

I held back uncertainly. "Maybe you'd better explain."

Elaine laughed. "He's been coming to our house a couple nights a week. He and Joe are tearing apart our old van and putting it back together. They were in the garage when I left."

I shook my head. I remembered my prayer, "Lord, make me tough." I would have to face my problems without depending on Chris.

Gabriel and I even went to the spot where the pinkish-white, bell-shaped flowers grew and picked several. Carefully I flattened them between the pages of my Bible. Later I would use them to decorate a book marker.

And then, quite suddenly, August added a sparkle to life's edges. It was county fair time and everyone was going. Darryl was popping with excitement.

His best friend had raised a lamb as a 4-H project and to everyone's surprise it had come home with the coveted blue ribbon.

"He gets to go to state! He gets to go to state!" Darryl had chanted. From then on he eagerly chronicled every event in Curly T.T.'s life.

He stood at the kitchen table gulping great draughts of milk and shoving oatmeal cookies into his mouth.

"We washed Curly T.T. this morning and guess what? We put bluing in the water."

"Bluing?" I asked stupidly.

"Bluing. It brings out the white." He smiled, the milk making an adorable bubbly mustache. "I bet you didn't know that, did you?"

I shook my head. The telephone rang, rescuing me from my ignorance. It was for me. My heart did a deep thump as I recognized Chris's voice.

"It's state fair week, Melissa," he said in his old comradely manner. "Can you go?"

"Why—why—Chris, why haven't you called?" I blurted.

There was a pause. Then, "Melissa, I'd be a liar if I just said I was busy. There've been things—things inside me I needed to get straightened out."

"Chris, I'm sorry. You don't have to tell me if you don't want to."

"But I do want to. You are the one person that I want to tell all about it—but not over the telephone. Tonight? Six-thirty? It's a good hour's drive to Salem."

"Sure, Chris. And Chris," I added somewhat self-consciously, "There's something I want to tell you, too."

"Tonight, then. Good-bye for now, Melissa."

I put the receiver down softly, wondering if I could find the words I needed to share with Chris something of the answer to my prayer for toughening.

As it happened, we didn't even talk about it. There were too many other things to be discussed.

I sat in the car, looking at him as much as I dared without seeming to stare. He was wearing a soft gold T-shirt that set off his brown eyes and beautiful tan.

"It's mostly ingrained grease from the service station," he said when I mentioned it. He looked at me thoughtfully, "Since we're passing out compliments, I like that gold thing around your waist."

I squirmed uncomfortably, hoping he wouldn't guess how long it had taken me to decide to wear it. I had on a simple green T-shirt I had bought with my baby-sitting money. Its lines were plain, and the sleeves almost nonexistent. But there was a gold fleck through the green, and I wore a matching gold belt around my waist.

I was silent for awhile, just watching the fields and groves of trees slip by. Then Chris turned off the freeway. I looked at him, a faint frown furrowing my forehead.

He grinned. "I told you I wanted to talk. I know this place by the river—Pat's Acres. We can talk there."

I could feel my teeth suddenly biting my lips. "Please, Lord," I prayed, "help me not to mention Colleen. I've done too much of that."

The car stopped at the end of a long bumpy lane. There were other cars and people down at the river but Chris ignored them. He reached for my hand. "There's this rock. . ."

We clambered over rocks and past swimmers to the accompaniment of rushing water. Around the bend Chris reached up and pulled a vine maple limb aside to reveal a tall rock, wide and flat on top. Chris gave me a shove, then climbed up beside me. Behind us were the woods and beside us slid the river. A bird flew low over the water, away from us, and a chipmunk suddenly scolded. "Not very welcoming," I observed.

But Chris didn't smile. I could tell he was searching for words so I fell silent, watching the river swirl and slide around the boulders and small rocks.

"Melissa," he said suddenly, "will you forgive me?"

I stared at him. "I don't understand."

"About the night of the banquet—I was too critical—too judgmental. I think I wanted you to be the perfect Christian. Maybe I was even trying to take the place of the Holy Spirit in your life."

"I still don't understand."

"I should have let the Spirit do the guiding and convicting, but somehow I felt you were special—"

"Like I was your bundle?"

"My what?"

It was my turn to flounder. "Well—I read this book. I don't even remember which one, but in it, it said something about everyone having another person for a bundle, or maybe a burden—I don't remember. But everyone who's a Christian has one. You know—someone they're responsible for in a special way."

Chris was silent for so long, I began to feel squirmy inside again. I picked up a few pieces of gravel and tossed them into the river.

At last he said, "Special, yes, but a burden, no." He reached out and squeezed my hand and the squirmy spot turned into a warm glow. Then he was pulling me down the rock. "State Fair, here we come!"

Laughing, we raced each other to the car. Somehow on that rocky stretch of riverfront, our mood had changed. Only once, as we sped towards Salem, did Chris grow suddenly sober.

"I've been seeing a lot of Rocky—er, Joe."

A cold chill ran up my back. "I know."

"I'm sorry, Melissa. I know how you feel about him, but somehow I think he's my responsibility, or bundle, if you want to put it that way."

I swallowed hard. "How come?"

"I'm not sure. Something inside me seems to be drawn to him—"

"Does he—did you talk about me?"

"Not exactly." He gave me a long look out of the corner of his eye. "I just mentioned you'd had a bad time since your sister disappeared."

"What did he say?"

"Not much. I just casually mentioned I knew you lots better than your sister and that you had no idea where she was."

"Why did you mention that?"

He gave me a dancing look. "Just in case he was Colleen's Rocky, I wanted him to know where you stood. Anyway, we dropped it then and went on to other things." He grinned. "When guys are fooling around with motors they don't get into personalities much."

A convertible loaded with teenagers careened around us. They laughed and honked. Instantly our sober conversation was forgotten as Chris waved and stepped on the gas.

I smiled and smugly settled back in the seat. Why, here I was, Melissa Lloyd, going to the fair with the best-looking guy I knew, and I was wearing my favorite color and I knew from Chris's eyes it looked good on me. It was a perfect situation and I was going to make the most of it! We were going to have a blast!

And we did. We whirled on rides until we were breathless. We ate yards of hot dogs and bushels of swirly pink cotton candy and threw balls at elusive bottles for prizes that never quite materialized. Then we went to the animal barn to pay our respects to Curly T. T.

I had to admit he did look grand with his perfectly groomed wool. And he was sporting a blue ribbon. I told Chris about Darryl's connection with the prize-winning animal and how they used bluing to make him beautiful. Then we walked over to the main building with its various displays.

My tennis shoes were beginning to rub my heels. Chris looked at me with concern as I bent to rub them. "We don't have to go over," he said. "We can sit down somewhere if you're hurting."

I shook my head. "Mother really would be upset if I didn't tell her about the prize-winning roses, the quilts, and the jams and jellies. I'm okay."

It was fun. As always, I was amazed at the intricate quilt patterns and the dainty, handcrafted items. We wound around and around, and in and out of the booths. I stopped to admire a wonderful, huge macrame planter made with driftwood before we went over to look at the vegetable displays.

Even they were a rainbow of colors, delightful to see; shiny red and yellow tomatoes, green, crisp-looking cucumbers, perfect ears of golden corn.

"I wish I could paint it just like it is," I said, dazzled by it's picturesqueness.

Chris beckoned to me. "Speaking of paintings—"

We went into a gallery-like hall. There were paintings, photographs and lithographs. I was instantly drawn to a group of Oregon wildflower photographs. Intently, I tried to identify each one. I recognized tiger lilies, trilliums and violets. A stab of excitement coursed through me as I identified the pinkish-white flowers I'd privately named my "toughening" flower.

Chris touched my shoulder. "Melissa, look at this photo. Doesn't it seem as though she's stepping into a brand new world?"

I pulled my fascinated gaze away from the wildflowers. I took a deep breath as I almost seemed to enter the picture before me. It was dawn and the tide was out. Pinkish pools swirled among dark gray islands and sand bars. Sea gulls flew silently in the misty rays of the morning sun.

Barefoot-prints drew my eyes to the ocean's edge. There, just where the sand met the sea, a girl was stepping into the water to meet the white-capped waves. She was wearing jeans, and a little handkerchief of navy blue was tied over her blonde hair.

"Colleen!" I cried. And suddenly the enormity of what Chris had said penetrated my mind. "Oh, Chris," I sobbed, "Does this mean she's dead?"

Chris stared at me uncomprehendingly. "Melissa," he murmured, "it's only a picture. Don't cry."

But I couldn't help it. All the pent-up feelings of the weeks without word of my sister were tearing at me. Chris's arm went around my shoulder. Gently, he led me out of the exhibit room, away from curious eyes. Humiliation welled up inside me.

Chris found a bench beneath a big oak, in a corner that was somewhat apart from the crowd. He made me comfortable, and then shielded me from passersby. Great snuffling sobs tore at me. With all my might I tried to drown them. At last, I wiped my drenched eyes and looked up at Chris.

"I'm sorry," I said. "It's partly the heat and maybe not enough sleep—"

"And worry over Colleen," he added. "What was it about that picture that upset you so? Or was it something I said?"

I swallowed hard. "Didn't you see, Chris? That girl stepping into the ocean—looked just like Colleen from the back—her hair, and the way she tied her handkerchief on her head. I was sure it was Colleen." My voice trembled. "And then you said something about her stepping into a brand new world and for an awful moment I thought—I thought it was a sign. . . ."

I think I could have stayed there forever with Chris beside me. But the picture was tugging at me. I jumped to my feet.

"I have to look at it again," I said, hoping he'd understand. He nodded and together we went back into the art hall.

There was no doubt about it, it was a beautiful photograph. And there was something oddly familiar about it. I knew it wasn't just the girl.

"Chris, I've been there before. Those rocks, and the way the sand is—it's uncanny."

Chris wrote the name of the photographer on a scrap of paper. "I'll try to get hold of him and find out where this was taken. Maybe—wait here." He disappeared into the crowd.

I looked at the picture for a long time. The girl was so like Colleen I couldn't believe it wasn't her. And that beach—

Suddenly I remembered the pink sky and a dying day and footprints in the sand. "Driftwood Beach," I said right out loud.

The lady beside me smiled appreciatively. "It's lovely, isn't it?"

It's Driftwood Beach," I said. "I went there once with my sister."

"How clever of you to recognize it," the lady murmured. She wandered away but I stayed.

"I'm going there very soon," I said, but there was no one to listen. Only Colleen's back seemed to mock me, "Too late. Too late."

I turned away and wandered over to where a stupendous mountain reared its head into the clouds. It was there that Chris found me.

He was jubilant. "Guess what? I talked to the photographer who took the picture. It's—"

"Driftwood Beach," I chimed in.

"How did you know?" he gasped.

"I've been there. I remembered. Chris, how did you ever manage to talk to him?"

"The girl in the information booth knew him. He's from Salem."

"Did he say anything about the girl?"

Chris shook his head. "He's never met her—just saw her walking into the water and thought it might make a good picture."

"Chris," I searched for words. "I know it sounds silly but—I'm going to that beach. I have to."

Chris looked at me long and hard. "We'll go together," he said, "the day after tomorrow." He touched my hand. "Would you do something for me in the morning? Like come to the Richards' garage? I'd like you to meet Joe."

13 / A Hidden Note, a Hidden Fear

I lay in bed, too restless to sleep. Pictures of the evening's events whirled through my mind; bright vegetable displays, Chris's arm around me, the ocean picture tugging at me.

To keep my mind from unraveling completely, I switched on the light and reached for my Bible. I tried to concentrate, pulling out a scrap of thought, a stray idea. But it was no use. I found myself thinking of other things. At last I gave up and put it aside.

Then I reached for a romantic novel. Perhaps I could be caught away for a while into another world and lose the problems of my own. But tonight was different. I found myself reading the same paragraph over and over and having no idea what I'd read. I tossed the book aside and got up.

Draping myself in my blanket, I went into the living room. I wandered about, fingering the ceramic owls on the bookcase and idly reading the book titles. After a while, I curled up on the couch.

It was awful. At exactly midnight, the cuckoo clock I loved by day chimed the hour. Tonight it sounded like a trapped bird in the walled silence, calling again and again. All night I waited for the hours to strike, hating the sound, yet strangely fascinated.

With the pale flush of early dawn I got up and went into Colleen's room. I turned on the light and looked intently at her ocean picture. It was a peaceful scene, the beach stretching before my eyes with only a few eddies and tufts of grass to disturb its smoothness. Overhead sea gulls seemed to drift out to sea, while a solitary sand piper ran over the sand.

Without conscious thought, I slid my hand behind the picture. A folded piece of paper brushed my fingers. I pulled it out, my hands suddenly shaking.

The words leaped out at me, words that filled my heart with a wild hope. "Melissa, I love you. Someday I'll see you again. Love, Colleen."

Gabriel's cold nose pressed my leg. I knelt down, pulling his head into my arms. "Gabriel," I whispered, "Do you suppose she left the note behind this picture to try to tell me something? It couldn't be a coincidence! It just couldn't."

Her childhood love for the ocean, the picture at the fair, and now the note blended together in a glorious hope. I could sleep now. Gabriel and I padded back to the couch.

And that's where Dad and Mother found us sprawled together. I wakened quickly, eagerly. I must ask permission to go to the beach with Chris. "And if I don't get it," I mumbled to Gabriel, "I'll just go."

"What did you say, Dear?" Mother asked.

"Nothing."

"How come you slept in here?" Dad asked.

"I was restless," I admitted.

Mother looked at me intently. "Did you have a nice time at the fair?"

"Beautiful." I got up, Gabriel and the blanket both sliding to the floor. Gabriel stretched and walked with stiff dignity to the door. I ruffled his ears affectionately before I let him out.

"Dad," I said, "I have to go to Driftwood Beach tomorrow."

"*Have* to?" he questioned.

I was silent for a moment, wondering how much I should tell him. My hopes of the night had paled in the morning light and an uneasy fear of failure was pressing in. Suppose we didn't find Colleen?

I dreaded any more disappointment for my parents, especially Mother. I was noticing a change in her face. Her cheeks were thinner and tiny lines I hadn't noticed before were showing around her eyes. Dad, too, looked older, more withdrawn. His quick and ready smile I'd always loved, hadn't been very quick and ready lately.

"*Want* to," I amended.

Mother turned away. "I don't see how," she said. "I know it's silly, but I just can't bring myself to leave the house empty. I keep thinking, what if she calls? What if she comes home and no one's here?"

"I didn't mean with the family, Mom. Chris and I—"

Dad's chin jerked up. "Just the two of you, alone?"

I nodded. "We talked about it last night. He has an Aunt and Uncle living in Newport. We could stay there tomorrow night and—"

"Overnight!" Mother exclaimed. "Really, Melissa, I don't know. . . ."

"We'd be well chaperoned, Mother. Really we would. As soon as Chris gets off work tomorrow we'll leave and—"

"You have it all planned, then?"

I nodded, feeling miserable and rebellious. But I just had to go. And today I must go to Elaine's house and meet Chris—and Joe. The thought made fear bunch up in my stomach.

It was still there when I sat at the breakfast table, lingering over my toast and orange juice. I was thankful when Gabriel came in and pushed his blond head against my knees. Covertly, I slipped him the toast. After that it was easier to slowly sip my juice.

I tidied the living room, then shut Gabriel in my bedroom. "I'm sorry," I said, in answer to his pleading look. "You can't come. Elaine's cat is scared to death of dogs—"

Slowly I set off for Elaine's house. To distract myself from my fears I played the license plate game Dad had taught us when we were small.

A red car went by, license plate APF—A Pretty Fox; Always Pick Friday. It turned the corner. Another: DMS—Drive More Slowly; Doleful Music Sounds.

A pick-up slowed and turned: FFF—Fear Feels Funny; Fearful Folks Fail. Irritation welled up inside me. "That's enough of that," I muttered.

I reached Elaine's yard, and suddenly felt a longing for Gabriel. I wished I'd brought him in spite of Elaine's black and white cat, Sir Frederick, who was mincing to meet me now. I put my foot out and rubbed his shoulders companionably. He sprawled over onto his back, his white paws playfully grabbing my ankles.

"That's enough, Sir Cat," I said. I went around to the back door and knocked softly. Elaine opened it at once.

"Melissa!" she cried, "I'm so glad you came."

Sudden remorse that I'd not come before made me reach out and hug her. Then Leila was beside me. I dropped to my knees and took her into my arms. Elaine and I smiled at each other over the top of the dark head.

"Chris asked me to come," I confessed.

A pout puckered Elaine's lips. She smiled as she glanced around the kitchen. "Sometimes, when the house is a mess, I'd rather you didn't. But I've just cleaned this morning. Come on in!"

The kitchen was warm and comfortable, a contrast to the cold appearance on the outside. I sat down in a straightback green chair and looked around. Cheerful curtains with a mushroom design decorated the windows. A bold orange rug in front of the sink and another by the stove added a splash of brightness.

I smiled at Leila as she moved into the circle of my arms, cradling a Raggedy Ann doll. Carefully she snuggled up into my lap.

I turned to Elaine. "Chris said he and Joe would be working on Joe's car this morning—"

"They're in the garage, or maybe I should say the grease." Elaine giggled. She arched her eyebrows at me. "You came to see Chris?"

"Sort of," I mumbled. "He wanted me to meet your brother."

Elaine gestured toward a door at the rear of the kitchen. "The garage is out here."

I took a deep breath. A part of me longed to spill all my fears on Elaine, but I couldn't. To do that would only hurt, not help.

My heart started pounding and I swallowed hard. I pasted on a frozen smile and followed Elaine.

The smells of grease mingled with gasoline hit my nose as she opened the door. An old Volkswagen van with mismatched fenders teetered menacingly on blocks, its headlights leering at me. I tore my fascinated gaze away to observe two pairs of blue-jeaned legs sticking out from beneath it at odd angles.

"Joe, Chris, you have company," Elaine announced. One of the blue-jeaned legs jerked convulsively, another contorted rapidly and Chris emerged. His hair was untidy and grease smudges covered his face, but his eyes showed he was glad I'd come.

"Melissa," he smiled, "I want you to meet my new friend, Joe. Hey, Joe—"

To break the silence that followed, I got down on my knees and peered beneath the car. "Hi, Joe."

He merely grunted. "Chris asked me to come and meet you," I said, the words stumbling from my lips. "He wants us to be friends."

Friends? his look snarled, but his voice was different, "Nice meeting you."

Chris kicked Joe's foot playfully. "Why don't you come out," he said. "Melissa is really special."

I flushed, and the fear began to lift. But it seemed to be hovering just over my head. Then Joe was beside me, his bent head leaning toward me.

I swallowed hard. "There's something I've been wanting to say for a long time, Joe," I stammered. "I'm really sorry I was so unfriendly the first time I met you."

Joe ran the back of his greasy hand over his mouth. He shook his head in obvious bewilderment.

A prayer shot from my heart. *Oh, Lord, help me to handle this your way.* I reached out my hand and gently touched his shoulder. "I appreciate your not holding it against me," I said.

"Oh, that's all right," he mumbled.

Elaine came to our rescue. "Would you guys like some fresh oatmeal cookies? Leila and I were going to bake a batch, and with Melissa to help us, we should be done in a jiffy."

As we stepped out of the garage, she turned to me. "Oh, Melissa! That was beautiful, so beautiful!" She opened the cupboards and pulled out the ingredients and baking utensils. "Here's hoping these cookies will be too."

"They will be," I assured her.

Before long the kitchen was filled with the aroma of cinnamon and raisins, and we were at the kitchen table sampling the cookies. I watched Joe out of the corner of my eye. *He's only a plain ordinary boy,* I kept telling myself, *except for a certain tautness in his manner.* I was almost convinced.

All the while I felt Elaine watching me. I tried to see things through her eyes. But it was Chris's parting words at the gate that really put the pink clouds back beneath my feet.

"Melissa," he said, "thanks for coming. I'm proud of you." He squeezed my hand gently. "Tomorrow, it's Driftwood Beach."

14 / A Guiding Star

It was hard to leave for Driftwood Beach the next day. It took several phone calls and a list of do's and don'ts before Dad gave his final okay. Even then, I felt kind of bad about it.

Deep inside I knew Mother didn't want me to go. But once Dad gave permission she quietly set about fixing us a picnic lunch.

Mom really went all out. The delicious aroma of fried chicken, potato salad, and chocolate chip cookies tempted us from the basket in the back seat. Gabriel sat between Chris and me and kept turning his head to catch the scent.

Chris grinned at me. "Let's eat soon," he said.

But we waited so as to enjoy the smell of the sea around us while we ate.

It was a restful drive. We didn't talk much, but it didn't matter. I kept remembering how Dad had said, "If you can spend an hour in somebody's company without talking and not be bored, then, that person is a true friend."

I took a side glance at Chris. His fine hands were firm on the wheel; his curly hair framed a striking profile. Bored with Chris? Never!

There were a couple of bad moments—Once when we turned off the road, I thought I saw a white, low-slung car behind us. My heart jumped into my throat, but I kept silent. After yesterday, I wasn't about to risk anymore misunderstandings. Besides, it couldn't have been Joe. I'd made it a point not to tell anyone where we were going. Not even Elaine.

The other low moment came when we drove by a house recently gutted by fire. Black charred walls were a backdrop for sunflowers, their once golden heads black and drooping, their leaves withered and lifeless. *Colleen*, I thought, *Colleen. Has your bright liveliness been snuffed out like that? Is your golden head still upright and shiny, or is it—*

I pushed the ugly thoughts aside and looked instead at the

113

low hills before us. Already I could see the promise of sea mist pushing its fingers toward us.

We smelled it before we saw it. We turned a corner and it was there, waves sparkling in the sun, laughing at the cloud bank pushed low on the horizon.

We spread our picnic lunch on a grassy peninsula jutting out to the sea. Campfires spread their lazy smoke into the air and good smells of sizzling barbecues drifted by us.

"Look, Chris—that campfire below us. Its smoke spreads out like long hair under water. It looks like a part of the sea."

"Mermaid hair," Chris murmured. He took a bite of chicken. "*You* look like part of the sea and sky in that turquoise blue, Melissa."

I could feel myself flush. To cover it, I pulled out the cookies. "Chocolate chip cookies, anyone?"

"Not yet," Chris said. He took another piece of chicken. "Melissa, I hate to mention it, but I think there's been a white car following us. Did you notice?"

I turned startled eyes to Chris. "Once I thought I saw Joe's—"

Chris nodded thoughtfully. "So did I. Or maybe it's somebody that looks like him. Don't look so scared, Melissa. You remind me of a startled chipmunk about to turn and run."

"It was probably our imaginations," I said weakly.

"Probably. And even if it were Joe—it's a free country. I guess he could drive down here if he wanted to."

Restlessness began churning inside me. I jumped to my feet and started jamming napkins and paper cups into the empty salad bowl.

"Hey, I'm not finished yet," Chris protested. He tossed the chicken bones into the pile and reached for a cookie.

"Can't we have our cookies while we drive on?" I hesitated. "I'm sorry, Chris. I just want to get to Driftwood Beach as soon as we can."

"Sure thing." Quickly he helped gather up the things and carried them to the car. Gabriel howled in disappointment, and I dug out an extra sandwich for him. "Spoiled dog," I said lovingly.

Slowly we drove down the winding coastal highway. At least to me it seemed slow. I found it hard to concentrate on the scenery now. Driftwood Beach was pulling hard at me and I could hardly wait.

But suddenly the whole panorama was before us, the beach,

the setting sun and the gorgeous sea. Chris pulled over.

"Look," I exclaimed. "See those drifting clouds? They look like golden sea gulls flying!"

"Beautiful," Chris said reverently. "I love that pale apple green where the yellow blends with the blue. It doesn't look much like the photo though."

"That's because it's high tide. Just wait, you'll see." I pushed open the door. "I'm going to look over the beach."

Chris joined me. Together we walked toward the sunset. To onlookers, I'm sure we appeared to be just a guy and his girl enjoying the scenery. At that moment, I would have given a lot if life could have been so simple. But I brushed those thoughts aside, and concentrated on a golden head with a handkerchief half hiding its brightness.

"Maybe we should separate," I said hesitantly. "We could cover more territory."

"I wouldn't want to leave you alone," Chris protested.

I looked down at Gabriel bouncing at our feet. "I wouldn't be alone. I'd have my guardian angel."

A smile brushed his lips. But his eyes remained serious. "I wouldn't want anything to happen to you."

"Just for an hour? We could meet at the car before dark. It's perfectly safe."

"All right. I'll go to that bunch of houses over there." He gestured toward a cluster of summer homes to our right.

"And I'll comb the beach. Come on, Gabriel." I turned toward the sand. I looked back once. Chris was climbing the rocks to the road that ran between the houses. He looked toward me and waved. I waved back, hope suddenly blossoming anew. Between the two of us we were bound to find her! *But what if she wasn't here?* The doubt nagged again.

"If she *is* here, we'll find her," I said stubbornly. "Gabriel, find Colleen. Find my sister."

Gabriel's head jerked up. He stopped, his nostrils quivering. Then he was running across the sand. "Gabriel, wait!" I cried. He paid no attention. I began to run but in a few minutes I'd lost sight of him.

I kept running. Just about the time I thought I couldn't stand the aching pain in my lungs, I saw him. He had left the beach behind and was standing on top of a mound covered with coarse grass and wild cucumber.

I slowed to a walk, taking great gasping breaths. Gabriel waited patiently, silhouetted against the darkening sky.

As soon as I caught up to him, he turned toward the trees and
began running again. "Gabriel," I implored, "Wait!" But it was
no use. He was racing along a path with its edges gradually changing from grass to tall salal that brushed my arms. Juniper dwarfed
by the perpetual winds sprang out at me. "Gabriel!" I cried.

He had disappeared again. Doggedly I kept following the trail,
wondering where it would lead, when the gleam of a lantern made
me realize I had stumbled into someone's campsite. I hesitated,
peering through the evening gloom. Just ahead was an abandoned
house, half tumbled to the ground. I could see Gabriel in the doorway, his form dark against the light. I crept closer. Maybe
Colleen—

Gabriel turned and looked at me. Even in the uncertain light I
saw gladness leaping in his eyes. I let out a strangled cry as I recognized Joe standing with his back to me, bent over a Coleman
stove. Another boy was cutting a loaf of French bread with a
gleaming butcher knife.

Both boys looked around. I stepped backwards, stumbling
over the debris in the yard. They were both coming at me. Joe
grabbed my arm and dragged me into the room.

"Please!" I cried, "you're hurting me!" His breath was sour
with beer.

In the flickering lantern light his eyes looked cruel, and the
towering shadows bending over me heightened the impression. I
felt like screaming, but I didn't. Somehow I had the presence of
mind to start praying silently.

"So you came to us. And this time you're alone," Joe said.
"Well, now we can talk."

"There's nothing to say," I protested.

"You came here to find your sister," he stated flatly. "We
came here for the same reason. That's why we followed you."

"But how did you know I was coming?"

A taunting smile slid across his dark features. He gestured towards his companion. "Kurt and I wandered by your house. Your
little brother was on the fence. He was pretty excited. Told us
you'd gone to Driftwood Beach to get your sister. I guess you
didn't much keep your side of the bargain, huh?"

"But I didn't know if I'd find her," I cried, wondering how
Darryl had known. "I was only guessing!" I tried to explain about

the picture at the fair, but all I got was an unbelieving stare. His hand tightened on my arm.

"Let go!" I cried. "You're hurting me!"

A low growl rumbled in Gabriel's throat. The hair on the back of his neck had risen and his teeth were showing, gleaming in the light.

I knew then he'd made a terrible mistake. But I understood. It must have been Joe's scent he'd smelled on Colleen's sweater.

With a swift movement Joe shoved me backwards onto a low cot pushed into the corner. Momentarily I lost my balance and stumbled to my knees.

A streak of blond, and Gabriel was hanging onto Joe's arm. The butcher knife flashed in Kurt's hand. I screamed. Kurt's leg shot out and caught my angel, tossing him headlong out the door. The dog yelped in pain.

I scrambled to my feet. I bit. I clawed. I kicked. But it was no use. Their strong arms overpowered me, pushing me onto the cot.

"You'll pay for this!" I cried.

"Tell us where your sister is, and we'll let you go!"

"No! Even if I knew I'd never tell you! Never!"

I saw Kurt's eyes meet Joe's. Kurt rubbed his cheek thoughtfully. Sudden, furious gladness welled up inside me as I noticed the long, red, scratch marks running from his forehead to his chin.

"Wait'll she cools off," he said.

I tried to sit up but Joe pushed me down. "You're staying with us," he said.

"Get your hands off me," I snipped.

"Will you stay put if I do?"

I nodded dumbly. He let go of me, but, his eyes didn't. They bored into me, challenging me to move.

I lay still. Gradually the details of the room pressed themselves into my consciousness.

The lantern sat on the table that was really a door propped on some pieces of rough lumber. A case of beer cans lay near the lantern. This room had obviously been a kitchen, for I could make out cabinets and a dirty sink in the dim flickering light. Kurt was heating soup on the Coleman stove placed on the filthy countertop. He offered me a cup and I took it reluctantly. Afterwards, I was glad I had. It warmed me considerably and I felt new courage well up inside. Then I noticed other details of the room; an old stuffed chair with its springs and padding poking out, the heaped up refuse on the floor between me and the door, the open window above me.

A breeze from the window made goose pimples bump up on my arms. I shivered and wished for my sweater in the car. I sat up and announced, "I'm going to sleep." Then I pulled off my tennis shoes and crawled into the sleeping bag on the cot.

Abruptly I turned my back to the boys. I heard their voices for a long time and then stillness descended. I shut my eyes tight and the only way I kept from going crazy with fear was by repeating all the Bible verses I'd ever learned. I started with John 3:16 and wandered all over, from Genesis' "In the beginning. . . ." to Revelation's "Behold I stand at the door and knock. . . ."

When I could tolerate my curled-up position no longer, I turned onto my back. Cautiously I turned my head—The lantern cast a low, uncertain light over the room.

I could just make out Joe's lumpy form beneath the table and Kurt, asleep in the big chair. I watched him. His head had fallen forward and every once in a while he made jerking movements and funny, big puffs of breath. I saw the glimmer of the butcher knife in his hand and shivered. Most definitely he was my guard, but a sleeping one. Or, maybe he was the sleeping giant, and I the defenseless Jack.

I looked out the window. A big star winked at me, the others paled in comparison. I watched it for a few minutes. *The wise men saw a star,* I thought. *They had followed it wherever it led.*

The star seemed to wink more brightly. As visions of Gabriel pushed in, the star grew large and blurry. And then I knew I was going to follow it, right back to the car. Now was the time. In a few minutes, Kurt might waken.

Cautiously, carefully, I pushed the sleeping bag back and slid out. My bare feet touched the rough boards. I bent over and picked up my shoes. Threading my way around the piles of debris, I kept one eye on the door, the other on my sleeping guard. Once he jerked and I froze, but then his slow breathing resumed. I was at the door, my heart lunging as I looked frantically for Gabriel's blond, motionless body. But there was nothing. The clearing stretched before my probing gaze. I didn't dare spend any time searching for Gabriel. At any moment my sleeping giant might arise and come after me. I slipped my shoes on.

"Forgive me, Gabriel," I whispered. I turned toward the star burning brightly above the ocean. Once again its brilliance misted, then shattered into splinters of light. I ran towards it.

15 / Driftwood Beach

I fled along the narrow path, away from my captors, toward the sands of Driftwood Beach—and Chris. Salal bushes scratched my arms and tore at my jeans. The sudden sound of pursuing footsteps made me freeze momentarily. I turned. Dark hulking shapes rose on the path behind me. *This has happened before*, I thought.

I left the path and ran through coarse grass. Sharp sticks and thistles stung my ankles but I scarcely noticed. I welcomed the smooth sand when I came to it. I was gasping for breath now and the wet sand clung hard to my soles. Over my own agonized breathing, I thought I could hear Joe and Kurt's. I tried to scream, "Chris!" but all I heard was my own rasping breath.

The wet sand dragged me downward and I fell forward. Shapes were coming at me. Hands were touching my shoulders. A cold nose pushed into my hand. I seemed to hear Colleen's voice crying, "Melissa! Melissa!" *I must be dying*, I thought, but no—there's no pain in heaven. I lifted my head.

"Colleen!" I cried, "Gabriel!" We were in each other's arms.

In the distance, I could hear Chris's voice angrily demanding of Kurt and Joe the meaning of their wild pursuit. I didn't hear their answer. I didn't really care.

My sister's arms were close around me and Chris was nearby. I knew he'd take care of everything.

"Colleen," I whispered, "Oh, Colleen, I've missed you so!"

Her arms tightening around me were her only answer. When I looked up I saw tears shining on her pale cheeks. *She looks older*, I thought. *I wonder—*

But my wondering would have to wait. Gabriel—my fingers touched his matted hair soaked with blood. "How could he do this to you?" I cried.

Then Kurt was there, arrogance vibrating from every line of his husky body. "I didn't mean to hurt him! I only meant to keep him from biting Joe!"

Chris touched my shoulder. "He's all right, Melissa. It's only a surface wound. Once he's cleaned up, you'll barely see it."

"He kicked him," I whispered, pulling Gabriel close into my arms.

I felt Colleen's fingers tighten on my arm. "What's going on?" she demanded.

"What's going on!" Joe exploded. "You have the nerve to ask that?" He stepped toward my sister, his dark eyes ominous, his lips a tightened pencil line.

Colleen's fingers quivered. But she kept her calm. "What's going on?" she demanded.

"The jewelry!" and his cry was like a lost animal, bereaved. "What have you done with my jewelry?"

I felt her cringe. "I did nothing with your jewelry!" she cried. "Don't you understand? That's why I ran away!"

"Colleen, Joe, you'll have to explain better than this," Chris said in a quiet, reasonable tone.

I looked at my sister. Her head was flung back, her hair gleaming in the moonlight. "You'll have to believe me. I ran because I couldn't stand the kind of person I was turning into. I was scared about the jewelry, Joe. So I wrote that letter and left it at the store for Mr. Reko to give to you—"

"What was in the letter?" Chris asked quickly. "Try to remember the words."

"Just—just—let me think. It was short. I said, 'Rocky, I'm sorry about the jewelry. I'm leaving. Don't try to find me,' or something like that. And then I left."

She looked at me in the moonlight. "I'm sorry, Melissa. I didn't want anyone to know where I'd gone. I didn't want any ties from the past. . . ."

I swallowed hard. I couldn't say anything.

"Let's go back," Chris said, "back to the jewelry. Joe, tell us about it."

Joe moved uneasily and I felt a sudden surge of pity for him. There was something so haunting in his eyes. I reached out and touched his hand. "Believe me, Joe, we want to help."

Joe cleared his throat. "It all started when I overheard Dad and Linda—she's my stepmother—talking. Linda was crying about how awful the place was and how she hated it. And then I heard Dad say he'd get some money from my mother's jewelry to fix it up.

"But it wasn't his to take and spend on Linda," he cried. "It was for Elaine and Leo and me! That was what mother wanted. So I broke the lock on Dad's strongbox, took the jewelry and hid it in my room."

He looked at Colleen. "That was about the time I met Colleen at the jewelry store. I'd gone in to sort of see how mother's jewelry compared—you know—just looking—"

Colleen nodded. "We got to talking, even went out for pizza a couple of times. Then he mentioned the jewelry. He was so afraid his dad would find out he'd taken it. Then he took me to his house to show me. It was so beautiful—so old and antique. We don't have anything to compare with it nowadays."

"She offered to put it in a safe at the store," Joe cried. "She said she'd show it to an appraiser and see how much it was worth. It wasn't really wrong, you see. It didn't belong to Dad or Linda. It belonged to us kids!"

"I got scared," Colleen continued. "Suppose Joe wasn't telling the truth. Even if he were, there was no proof his real mother wanted him to have it." She lowered her eyes. "There were other things, too. I was starting to hate myself. I felt like I was slowly being sucked under—and so I ran." She lifted her head and faced Joe bravely. "I'm sorry, Joe."

"But I took the jewelry to you like we'd planned!" he cried. "My brother saw you in the window after he let the bucket down—He filled it with sand so no one would guess—"

I gasped. "Then he saw me, Joe. I slept that night in her room."

"Then you *do* have the jewelry!"

"No!" I cried, "I've never seen it!"

"But it was in the bucket!"

"The bucket is gone! I took it out to the sandbox, and it disappeared."

Joe's head sank forward. "But I talked to Colleen the next day!"

"No, Joe. That was me. I just pretended to be Colleen. Just because—well, just because I thought I'd find a clue as to where she went. I—"

Chris broke in roughly. "Then you ransacked Colleen's room, didn't you? And you left a threatening note for Melissa at the store—"

"I was afraid she'd go to the store before I got a chance to check the safe—if I could. And then I thought maybe she was telling me the truth, that she wasn't Colleen. I mean—"

"Then you went into her room," Chris said in a low, hard voice, "and scared her to death—"

"You don't understand! I had to find that jewelry. I had to—I still do!"

"Well," said Chris briskly. "At least now we know what we're looking for. The jewelry was in a bucket; the bucket went to the sandbox, and then disappeared."

"Wait!" I cried, "Let me think!" Crazy mixed-up thoughts marched through my brain. Somehow I knew I had the pieces to the puzzle but couldn't grasp them. I looked at Chris and Joe. "Just give me a minute," I pleaded.

My fingers pushed deep into Gabriel's soft hair. The waves pounded on the shore. I looked up at the moon, round, golden. *The bucket—Darryl—"I'm a pirate!" he'd cried. And then, "I didn't take her sweater. But I took something else. I buried it where Gabriel will never find it."*

A whisk of clouds scuttled across the moon's golden fullness. *Darryl on the fence. Something gold gleaming over one eye, a chain encircling his head.*

"Joe," I asked, "was one of those jewelry pieces a gold pendant on a chain?"

"I thought you said you never—"

"I didn't, or at least I didn't know then what it was!" I looked around at the waiting group. "No," I said, "I didn't take them, but I think I might know where they are."

Excitement sparked Joe's eyes. "Where!" he cried.

"I think my little brother buried them."

"What!" they all cried.

"I'm not sure," I explained. "He said he hadn't seen the bucket when I asked, but I think he—"

"Let's find out right now!" Joe cried, springing forward. Chris detained him with a shake of his head.

"It's late, and I'm sure since it's waited this long, another day won't make much difference. Besides, my aunt and uncle will probably think we've been in an accident, and Melissa needs to clean up."

I looked down at my tattered clothes ruefully. "She can stay at my house." Colleen said quickly.

Chris nodded. "Joe and Kurt can come with me."

The boys exchanged looks. I saw Joe shrug and then nod at Chris.

"We're already camped back there," Kurt said, jerking his thumb in a general direction.

"Just the same, you're coming with me."

Frantically I tried to get Chris's attention. "They have a butcher knife," I said. "That's what hurt Gabriel. They threatened me with it."

"Well?" Chris said.

Kurt drew back his shirt and tossed the knife to the sand. "I wouldn't have hurt anybody," he said.

Chris picked up the knife thoughtfully.

"I think you owe my sister an apology," Colleen snapped.

"Sorry," grunted Kurt.

But Joe was more articulate. He extended his hand. "I really am sorry, Melissa. I was scared half out of my head, but that's no excuse. I'm sorry I took Colleen's sweater and necklace. I did it for spite, I guess."

I touched his arm. "I hope we find the jewelry," I said. And I meant it.

We walked to Colleen's house in the moonlight; Gabriel was close behind, followed by the boys. I was glad the world was asleep, for an odder assortment of young people I've yet to meet. Me, in my torn T-shirt and rumpled jeans; Kurt and Joe, dirty, disheveled; Chris so very much in control of the situation; and Colleen, her blonde head high, her dark corduroy jacket immaculate. Beside us trotted Gabriel wearing his battle scars proudly.

We came to a little summer home huddled all by itself in an unexpected crevasse—or so it seemed in the moonlight. Light through its wide windows beamed forth a golden welcome. It illumined what looked to be a bevy of sea gulls perched at random on posts and driftwood pieces. The boys left us there, with a promise to return in the morning.

As Colleen and I walked up the path, a bird thrust its beak close to my face. I shrieked and drew back. Colleen laughed.

"It's not alive," she explained. "They are my cement menagerie, but I only paint them. A lady in Newport does the pouring."

I reached up and touched an outspread wing. "You always did have a weakness for sea gulls, didn't you."

"Always." She went ahead to the door. "Come in. Welcome to my humble abode."

I looked eagerly around the lamp-lit room. There were no chairs or couches, only bright cushions scattered in front of a low fireplace and a coffee table pulled close. The rest of the room was devoted to art, an easel by the window, paints and paintings everywhere, against the wall, on the floor.

My attention was captured by a large unframed painting over the fireplace. It was Driftwood Beach caught in the glory of a pink sunset. Waves reflected candy-pink clouds. Figures on the beach had a pinkish glow and so did their tiny footprints. I saw the pink jet trail disintegrating into pink powder.

"You remembered," I said.

Colleen smiled. "Did you think I'd forget? Melissa, there's a shower off the bedroom. I'll put something out for you." She disappeared into an alcove off the living room. "I'm making hot chocolate," she called.

Before I cleaned up, I washed the blood off Gabriel's head. Chris was right. The cut was barely noticeable.

As I showered, I thought I could have stood forever letting the warm water pound its healing through me. But I wanted to talk to Colleen, so I turned it off and quickly dried myself. Then I slipped into the soft green flannel gown Colleen had laid on the bed.

A small fire was burning in the front room. I went over and knelt before it, holding my hands to the softly whispering flames. Colleen came in with foaming mugs. She had changed into a dark blue corduroy robe that hugged her figure closely. "You're thinner," I observed.

She smiled and pulled a cushion close to the fire and sat down. "Okay," she said, "now we can talk. What do you want to know?"

I spread my hands helplessly, "*Why*, Colleen—just *why*? I know what you said on the beach, but I don't understand—not really."

"It's hard to explain something you hardly understand yourself." She took a sip of the chocolate. "Of course, it wasn't just the jewelry. It was my entire life. All I wanted to do was run from this guy to that, and each one was a little bit lower. . . ."

I flushed, and lowered my eyes.

"You read my diary, didn't you, Melissa?"

"Yes," I whispered, "but nobody else did. Not even Mom—"

"Melissa, don't look so worried. It doesn't matter, not now. Maybe deep inside I left it because I wanted you to find it— that you might understand something of the hell I've been going through."

"But Colleen, how could you? We were so worried."

"How are they, Mom and Dad and Darryl?"

"All right. But Mom's face is different. Dad doesn't say much, he's changed. Oh, Colleen, why didn't you get word to them? Why didn't you tell them where—"

Colleen leaped to her feet. "Because they were part of the reason I was running away! Their love was like a leash! It was always do this, you *should* do that! Why, if I'd told them I was going they'd have very gently and reasonably talked me out of it! I had to break away—had to be myself without anyone interfering! I wanted to be free to be me!"

"But now you'll—"

"No! I'm not going back. Not yet. I need time. I'm building a new life. I'm trying to put God back in the place He had when I was a little girl. I'm not ready yet."

She sank back down on her cushion. "I'm making it on my own now, Melissa. Just barely, but making it. I'm painting pictures and just last week I sold my first one. I help this lady with her sea gulls and she pays me a little. And there's a little church in town I'm starting to get involved in.

"Of course, I couldn't make it if it weren't for Pete; he owns this cabin. He's a Christian guy. Hey, don't get the wrong idea— he's in the coast guard now. He lets me stay without paying rent."

"Where did you meet him?"

"At Reko's store. We even went to church together while he was on leave. I talked to him about my drawing and how lost I felt just going to the store everyday and smiling at Mr. Reko and his customers and doing a bit of typing. And then running, every night—running, running. It just wasn't me, and he understood. Right out of the blue he told me if I ever wanted to stay here while he was gone, I could. I think he figures it's a good investment. In fact, that's what he said, 'a good investment for the Lord.' So when this thing with Joe got out of hand, I just took off and came here. I've not been sorry."

I was silent. The months of anguish at home were something she would never understand. What was it her girlfriend had once told me? Ah, yes. "Colleen will never have ulcers. She'll just give them to everyone else."

"Of course," she continued, "there've been days when all that was in the refrigerator were a couple of eggs—and a box of cereal on the shelf—"

"If you need money while you're starting, I'll ask—"

"No, Melissa, you still don't understand. This is something I must do on my own, with no one's help but God and—"

"And Pete," I said, trying to keep the bitterness out of my voice.

"Yes—Pete. Somehow I think he was heaven-sent. But Melissa—there's something in your voice. We're not communicating."

"Mom and Dad—" I choked on the words.

"What about them? So they miss me. Well, after all, I am almost twenty!"

"They *love* you," I whispered. "Love doesn't pay any attention to age."

"But I did call the night of the storm. I was so afraid! But I was cut off!"

We fell silent. It was hard to swallow the chocolate cooling in the cup. Numbly I put it aside and walked to the window. The sand and sea stretched before me. But it was empty, barren.

I heard Colleen behind me. "Melissa, all my life people have called me 'Sunshine,' 'Miss Sunshine,' 'Sunny,' whatever. And all my life I've been trying to catch its glow but somehow never able to get my eyes off the ground. Melissa, help me!"

I turned to her then. Our arms encircled each other and we both cried. "Melissa, I've been so confused. I've cried over the wrong things and wanted the moon. But I wouldn't have known what to do with it if I'd gotten it. Forgive me."

Then sleep came and after that the dawn. We stood together at low tide and watched little swirls of coffee-colored islands reflect the early rays. And I told her about the picture and how we'd come to Driftwood Beach.

Then she told me how Chris had seen a girl looking out to sea who had her hair and figure. He'd called, "Colleen!" But, when he'd come closer he saw she wasn't Colleen after all. Having been mistaken for Colleen before, the girl offered to bring him to Colleen's house. And that's how he found her.

They returned to the car, but found only Gabriel there. His head was bloodied and he was barking wildly. Quickly they followed him along the beach until they spotted me.

"Melissa, you'll never know how glad I was to find you, wild pursuers and all."

We laughed and then grew thoughtful. "Can you see God's hand in all this, Colleen? How He's led each step of the way?"

"In even more ways than you know, Melissa. My paintings, my sea gulls, Pete—and Chris. He likes you, doesn't he?"

My cheeks flushed to match the dawn. "That picture—the one of him by the lion. Where did you get it?"

"His sister. She knew I had a crush on him but he'd never even look at me. She gave it to me one day; she'd taken it for photography class in our senior year. And then she'd said, 'Just look and dream, but remember, he's saved for somebody special.'" Colleen's smile was quick and loving. "That someone special must be you."

"Oh, Colleen," I said doubtfully.

"If it ever happens, Melissa, remember, here's one sister who'll be delighted."

Then we were running across the sand, around the little islands, jumping over the rivulets of water trickling back to the ocean. And sea gulls were flying and sandpipers were piping. And that was the way it was when the boys found us.

I didn't have the chance to tell Colleen before I left how much I'd found out about myself that summer, that finally I knew where I was headed. Nor had I shared how "waiting" on God's Word was changing me. That would have to come later.

Her address was safely tucked in my jeans pocket and beside me on the seat rested a painted sea gull. Just as we were leaving, she'd slipped it into the car.

"It's for Mother and Daddy," she'd explained. "Tell them I love them and to please try to understand. And, Melissa, please ask them to give me time. . . ."

As our car pulled away, I turned and looked back. I couldn't tell for sure, but I think she was crying.

16 / Hidden Treasures

I stepped into the kitchen, the heavy sea gull in my arms. "Mother!"

She scarcely looked up, so deeply absorbed was she in the tomato sauce bubbling on the stove. I sniffed the spicy goodness and waited.

She dipped a spoon into it and held it out to me. "Do you think the spices are right or should I add a bit more cloves?"

I touched its hot goodness cautiously with my tongue. "It's just right, Mother."

For the first time she noticed me, really noticed. "Melissa, you're home early!"

I nodded, wondering how to tell her that I knew Colleen's whereabouts. My thoughts tumbled: *Lord help me. And help Mother to understand so she won't rush off and undo everything Colleen has just begun to let you do in her life.*

"What is that you're hugging?" Mother asked.

"It's a sea gull. A gift for you—and Dad."

"For me? Why, Honey, where did you get it? These garden statues are expensive."

"It's not from me. It's from—Colleen." And I dumped the large unwieldy bird into Mother's arms.

"Colleen! How—"

I put my arms around her. "She's all right, Mother. In fact, she's better off now than when she was home."

"But where—"

"In a little house by the beach—Driftwood Beach."

Mother sat down suddenly. "Is she coming home?"

"Not now, Mother. Later. I'm sure she will later."

"Then your Dad and I must—"

I touched her arm. "*No*, Mother. She asked that you not come. *Not yet.*"

Mother's lips quivered. To my dismay I saw tears suddenly

well up in her eyes. "Mother!" I cried. Her face crumpled. My arms went around her shoulders. I pressed my cheek in her hair.

"Mother, she loves us all very much. It's just that right now she's trying to make a life for herself without our interfering. Later, when she really finds out where she's going, she'll be back. I know she will."

Mother reached for a tissue. When she spoke, her voice was steady. "How did you know where she was, Melissa? You did know, didn't you?"

"It was sort of a guess, but not entirely." I told her about the photograph at the fair and the note behind the picture in Colleen's room. "It wasn't much, but it was something."

"And she doesn't want to see us yet. . . ." It was a statement, not a question.

"Let me explain it the way she told me." I searched for words. "She wants to start a new life that is really hers. And she wants God to be in charge of it. She said she was drifting in the wrong direction here at home and she didn't know how to get started back in the right direction.

"And she is, Mother. I mean, she's at least starting. You should see her paintings. She sold her first one. She helps a lady by painting gulls like this one she sent you and Daddy."

"But how can she live? I mean—"

"A Christian man lets her stay in his beach cabin rent-free while he's gone. All she has to do is earn enough to eat on. She must be doing all right. After all, she's still alive!" I couldn't bring myself to tell her how thin Colleen was. That could come later, if at all.

Mother got up briskly. She handed me the sea gull.

"Mother," I said hesitantly, "Could I call Dad at the office?"

She nodded. I followed her to the phone. Uncertainly, I picked up the receiver, and dialed slowly.

"Dad," I swallowed hard, "Dad—it's me, Melissa. I—I—Colleen's safe, Daddy—I found her."

There was total silence; then, "Thank you, Lord—Thank you, Melissa." Sudden tears burned my eyes as I handed Mother the receiver.

"Wait, Melissa," Mother said. "Would you please take the gull to the garden and put it at the end of the path? We'll talk more later—"

I went outside and up the path. I knew why Mother wanted it

there. It would welcome Dad home and assure him of Colleen's love.

I settled the sea gull onto a piece of driftwood and stepped back. It seemed to be at home and I was pleased.

A sudden yell startled me, and a small "catapult" charged at me. "Melissa! Melissa! Where is she? Where is she?"

I caught Darryl firmly around the waist. "Hey, slow down! You and me, we've gotta talk."

He stood there, his hair sticking out in all directions, his eyes wide and expectant. "Where is Colleen?" he demanded. "Why didn't you bring her home with you?"

"Tell me something, young man. Why did you tell people I was going to find her? Did you read my diary?"

He wilted visibly. "Just that little bit—you know, how you wrote about God being such a close friend you could tell Him everything and He'd hear you. And then that last page about how you felt you were pulled to Driftwood Beach; that you were sure Colleen was there."

He lifted his head defiantly. "I figured if you could talk to God and ask Him anything, I could too. So I just asked God to let you find Colleen."

I hugged my little brother close. "I did find her, Darryl. I did. She didn't want to come home with me right now, but she will later."

I told him about the little cabin with windows that open to the sea and sea gulls in the yard. And about Colleen's paintings that would hang in homes—far and wide. "And someday," I concluded, "when her thinking is all straightened out and she really finds herself, we'll go see her."

Surprisingly Darryl seemed to understand more easily than Mother had. "Do you think she'll remember me when she's ready?" he asked.

"Of course she will!" I paused, "Darryl, there's something else that needs to be straightened out. Somebody's missing some jewelry. It was in a bucket and it disappeared."

He nodded. "Yup, I know. I'm sorry I lied about it when you asked me before. But I was having so much fun—I buried them, you know."

My heart lurched. "They're very valuable, Darryl. Do you remember the place?"

He scratched his head thoughtfully. "I think—well—I moved

them from place to place, you know, playing pirate."

"Can you find the spot, Darryl? I need to take them back to their rightful owner."

"Who's that?"

I hesitated. "You know Elaine. They're her family's."

"Oh, I'll go get the shovel." And he was gone, racing around the back of the house.

Suddenly I wanted Chris to share this moment. "Wait!" I called, "I'm going to call Chris."

The three of us gathered beneath the spreading branches of an old oak tree in the woods that bordered our house. The sun, swinging low through the afternoon, shown in slanting rays through the branches, sliding its fingers through Chris's dark hair, and highlighting a solitary leaf which rested there for an uncertain moment before fluttering to the ground. *Bits of September,* I thought; and sudden bittersweet sadness tinted the afternoon. Change was on the way. Chris would soon be leaving for college.

He was kneeling where freshly disturbed dirt marked the spot. "Was it here?" he asked my brother.

But Darryl looked confused. "I kept moving it," he said.

"Think, Darryl," I urged.

Chris grabbed the shovel. "We can at least try. In the meantime, you put on your thinking cap, young man."

Several rapid shovelfuls revealed nothing. "Wait," Darryl said. "Now I remember." And he was gone, crashing through the underbrush.

Chris and I looked at each other in quiet desperation before plunging after him. Hazelnut branches slapped our faces and wild blackberry brambles tore at our clothes.

"Darryl, isn't there a better way?" I yelled.

"No," he called back. "Come on! We're almost there."

We climbed over several low vine maple branches before emerging into a clearing. Darryl was standing in the middle. Determinedly he started walking. "1, 2, 3, 4, 5 steps." He stopped and stuck both arms out like airplane wings, then did a sharp right. "1, 2, 3, 4, 5. Here it is!"

Chris and I were at his side in a bound. I gave Darryl a withering look. "Are you sure?"

But Darryl was undaunted. "If I could dig, please."

Chris handed him the shovel. In a moment we heard a suspicious clink. Darryl dropped the shovel and began pushing the dirt aside with his hands. Chris and I dropped to our knees and began helping. Even Gabriel got into the act and the dirt flew. But it was Darryl who lifted out the battered sand bucket. His eyes shone as he handed it to me.

I took it with trembling hands. Carefully I pushed the dirt out, and started to pour the sand on the ground.

"Wait," Chris said. "We don't want to lose a single piece." He took off his shirt and laid it on the ground.

Gently I upturned the bucket and there they were in reality, the glittering splendor of Colleen's picture. I recognized the gold tiara, the pendant, the brilliant emerald necklace, the amethyst bracelet.

"The star pin," I whispered. "It isn't here."

"It's in your room," Darryl volunteered. "It's been there all the time."

"My room!" I cried. "Where?"

"Under your bed. I laid on my back on the floor and stuck it into the springs."

"Well that's that," Chris said. "Let's gather these up and take them to Joe and his family." He gripped Darryl's shoulder. "Thanks a lot, pirate. You did a terrific job of keeping these jewels safe."

Carefully, we removed the sand from the shirt and wrapped up the jewelry. Darryl picked up the empty bucket. "I'm going to miss them," he said wistfully.

Miss them? And yet as I looked at the bucket, I knew that somehow I would miss the excitement, the mystery, the thrill of sharing with Chris something that had drawn us together as nothing else could have.

I reached down and rumpled Darryl's hair. "I'm going to miss them too," I said.

Gabriel threw his head back and howled.

17 / Return of the Star

Three bedraggled treasure hunters trooped into the Richards' kitchen. Bits of twigs stuck every which way out of Darryl's tousled sun-streaked hair, Chris was shirtless but triumphant. And I—I felt at a decided disadvantage with my shoulder sticking out of my briar-torn shirt.

But Joe's eager cry when he saw the sand bucket in Darryl's hand distracted me. "You've found them!"

Before we could answer, he reached for the bucket. "They're gone! Gone!" The bucket crashed to the floor. Joe's hands came up and covered his face.

"Hey, wait!" Chris cried. He spread his shirt on the table.

Joe uncovered his face; Elaine and Leila gathered close. Once more they lay in glittering splendor; red ruby mingled with green emerald, the gold of the tiara, the pale blinking amethyst.

"Ooh," Elaine exclaimed. "It's the ruby necklace." She picked it up, rubbing it gently.

Joe leaned forward and picked up the amethyst bracelet, looping it around his fingertips. "They've been in the family for years," he murmured. "How can we ever thank you?"

Darryl stood up. "You can thank me by giving me an oatmeal cookie," he said. "Melissa says they're great."

Everyone laughed. Leila came forward and shyly held her hand out to Darryl. He took it solemnly, and she led the way to the cookie cannister.

Elaine picked up the rosy coral bracelet and laid it against her cheek. "It's so smooth—so beautiful—"

Joe started to reach for it, then stopped. "The star pin!" he cried. "It isn't here!"

Darryl turned around, his mouth full of cookies. "It's under Melissa's bed," he volunteered. "We forgot to bring it. I'll get it for you."

"Under Melissa's bed?" Joe exclaimed. He scowled at me in

the old menacing way, but this time I only smiled. "It was Darryl's little game," I said. "It was he who put it there."

"She didn't know," Chris explained.

"But you're sure of it?" Joe demanded.

"I'll get it," Darryl insisted. Leila stepped behind him and pushed another cookie into his hand. He shoved it quickly into his pocket and ran to the door. "I'll be back in a little while!" he cried.

Joe took a deep breath and rocked back on his heels. "I sure hope it's there," he muttered.

"I suspect it's been a lot safer than this buried treasure," Chris observed somewhat tartly. "He'll bring it back."

Elaine stood up. "Would you like some cookies?"

I smiled up at her, my stomach feeling empty. "Yes," I said, "please."

Joe leaped to his feet. "There's Seven-Up in the fridge. I'll get it."

We were at the table munching cookies and sipping Seven-Up when the door opened. A dark boy with a baseball bat swung over his shoulder came in. "Umm, cookies," he exclaimed and made a grab for the plate.

Elaine stopped him with a, "Just a minute, little brother. I've got friends for you to meet."

He smiled sheepishly and glanced around the table. "I know you from somewhere," he said as he looked at me. "You're—" His smile deepened and I saw pure white teeth in contrast to his tanned face.

"You're Leo," I said slowly. "We've met before—Remember a window in the night, an old sand bucket—"

"Oh, yeah, I do—I do!"

He spotted the bucket lying upturned on the floor. "Hey, there it is! What is this anyway?" He looked at Leila contentedly playing with the jewelry on Chris's shirt. He shook his head in puzzled amazement.

Elaine reached into the cupboard for another glass. "Chris, this is Leo. Leo, Chris. And that's Darryl," she said as he popped in the door.

Leila jumped up and ran to him. It was to her that Darryl presented the star pin. She took it carefully, her lips puckering into an O. I sucked in my breath in anticipation but no sound came. Instead she walked around the room, holding the pin in her palm, tilting it at different angles.

"She's catching the colors from the sun's reflection," Elaine whispered.

I nodded. "She's beautiful," I murmured. "It's positively captivated her, hasn't it?"

"She loves colors, patterns. Sometimes I think she sees things that I don't," Elaine said.

I pushed my chair back and went over to Leila. Gently I touched the star points, the intricate filigree. "See, Leila. It's pretty, pretty—"

But Leila only nodded. Silently we watched the light from the window reflect green and red from the gleaming surface.

"Star," I whispered, "a star for you, my little Star Flower."

A light flashed in Leila's eyes. "Star," she whispered, "star—for you." And Leila laid the pin in the palm of my hand. A lump filled my throat. I felt Elaine's hand on my shoulder. "Oh, Melissa, she's talking, talking—"

Then Chris put his arm around me and hugged me close. But Leila seemed unaware of the feelings she had evoked. She ran to Darryl and the two rushed again to the cookie jar. "Filling their stomachs again," Joe commented huskily.

I put the pin into his hand. He looked at it a long time, his dark eyes thoughtful, caught away in his own world. I wondered what he was thinking.

"We should go," Chris said.

I pushed my glass aside and called Darryl. At the door Joe stopped me, his hand heavy on my shoulder. "I'm not very good with words," he said awkwardly, "but I—I think Chris was right when he said you were special."

Chris and I walked home in the blazing sunshine with Darryl racing ahead.

"It's been a perfect day, hasn't it?" he said.

I nodded. "And to think that star pin was there under my bed the whole time and I didn't even know it!"

"I know what you mean," Chris said thoughtfully. "It's that way with things in the Bible too. You know, there're beautiful truths there, but somehow we don't always see them. At least not always right away."

"It's sort of like hidden treasure, maybe," I said. "We have to dig—

"Oh, Chris! This morning before Colleen was awake I was reading about Esther in the Persian palace. All of a sudden it hit me. Why, there she was, ready and available, making herself beautiful, getting ready to go to the king.

"Then at the banquet she held back, waiting to see how the king would handle her problem. Yet all the time she was looking forward expectantly. She knew that God wouldn't let His people perish."

A sudden thought struck me. "Chris! Esther means star! And today was the day the star returned! Isn't that beautiful?"

Chris smiled at me. "Yes, it is beautiful," he said.

But somehow I had the distinct impression he wasn't thinking of Esther at all. I jabbed his ribs with my elbow and ran ahead.

The next night Chris and I walked together in the woods where the jewelry had been hidden. We paused beneath the oak, only this time it was the moonlight that gleamed in his hair.

I looked up to the star I fancied was the one I had followed the night I had run away from Joe.

"Chris, I want to show you something." I held out the star pin. He took it gently, the moonlight catching its intricate silver filigree.

"Mr. Richards called this afternoon," I said. "He said Joe and Elaine, even Leo and Linda, wanted me to have it as a reward for helping find the jewelry—But I'm not going to keep it.

"I'm going to pin in on my drapes as a reminder to me to keep following my true Star, Jesus, and the new goals He's given me. Then when Leila is older I'm going to give it to her. You know, I've always called her Star Flower in my mind. Maybe by then she'll know who the Bright and Morning Star is."

"That's a great idea. I have something for you, too. It's not valuable like your star, but—well—it'll be sort of a reminder of what we've been to each other this summer. I brought it with me to help me say good-bye."

"Good-bye?"

He nodded. "I have to leave day after tomorrow. An after-school job I applied for is available early. I have to go—it's a good job and the wages are great for part time. . . ."

He opened my fingers and then closed them over something soft and feathery. "It's a little sea gull covered with real feathers. I want you to keep it and always remember."

I looked at him in the moonlight. His eyes were tender and I had to fight a sudden longing to touch his lips with my fingertips.

To distract myself, I looked at the moon behind him. A big cloud was racing towards it. It looked like a lion with streaming mane and tail. And then it changed into a knight.

For a moment his floating cape blotted out the moon's brightness, and Chris took me gently into his arms. The curious oak above us could only whisper its suspicions to the forest.